ANNALS OF RAJASTHAN
ANNALS OF MEWAR

ANNALS OF RAJASTHAN
ANNALS OF MEWAR

C. H. PAYNE, TOD

GYAN

Published by

Gyan Publishing House
5, Ansari Road
Daryaganj, New Delhi-110002
Phone: 011-47034999, 9811692060
E-mail: books@gyanbooks.com

Distribution Network
gyanbooks.com
India, USA, Canada, UK, Australia, France

ISBN : 978-81-2123-131-2 (PB)

2nd Impression 2020

Printed at: Gyan Press, Delhi.

Annals of Rajasthan Annals of Mewar
Author: C. H. Payne, Tod

Photo by] [*Donald Macbeth, London*

MAHÁRÁNA BHÍM SINGH.

Frontispiece

ANNALS OF RAJASTHAN

THE ANNALS OF MEWAR

ABRIDGED AND EDITED BY

C. H. PAYNE, M.A.

LATE OF THE BHOPAL STATE SERVICE

With 16 full-page Plates and a Map

LONDON

GEORGE ROUTLEDGE & SONS. LIMITED

BROADWAY HOUSE. 68-74 CARTER LANE, E.C.

Preface

"WHEREVER I go, whatever days I may number, nor time nor place can ever weaken, much less obliterate, the memory of the valley of Udaipúr." Such are the words with which Colonel James Tod closed his great work, the *Annals and Antiquities of Rajasthan*. Few men have ever known an eastern race as Tod knew the Rájpúts. He not only knew them through and through, their manners, their traditions, their character, and their ideals; but so great was his admiration for their many noble qualities, and so completely did he identify himself with their interests, that by the time he left India he had almost become a Rájpút himself. The history of Rájpútána was, therefore, a subject very dear to Tod's heart; and, possessing both imagination and descriptive power, he was able to infuse into his pages much of the charm of a romance, and, what is still more rarely to be found in historical works, a powerful human interest. His sympathy for the Rájpúts is apparent in every line he wrote; but if his enthusiasm leads him at times to overestimate their virtues, he never seeks to palliate their faults, to which, in the main, he attributes the ruin which overtook their race. Notwithstanding its author's occasional inaccuracies, and the somewhat glaring defects of his style, the *Annals and Antiquities of Rajasthan* still holds its place as the standard authority on the history of the Rájpútána states. Of subsequent writers of Indian history, it would be difficult to point to a single one who has not benefited directly or indirectly by Tod's labours. But however great the value of the "Annals," viewed in the light of an historical record, they owe their chief charm to the vivid pictures they present of the character, sentiments, and heroic exploits of one of the bravest races that ever came under British control, and of the manner in which that control was established. Rájpútáná has passed through a century of progress since the "Annals" were written. But it must be remembered that, in our eastern Dependency, habits of life have undergone a much greater change than national prejudices and national ideals; and hence it is that, for those who would understand the India of to-day, there is no surer guide than the past history of her peoples. Of the thousands of books that have been written about India, few reveal her secrets more faithfully than the *Annals and Antiquities of Rajasthan.*

And yet this great Indian classic is practically unknown to the present generation, and is all but unprocurable. The first edition, contained in two quarto volumes, and illustrated by a number of steel engravings of high quality, was published by Messrs Smith, Elder & Co. between the years 1829 and 1832. This is the only edition ever published in England, and it has long been out of print. A second, in two octavo volumes, but without the illustrations, appeared in Madras in 1873; and a third of a similar nature, but less accurate, in Calcutta in 1894. The two latter are likewise out of print, and hard to come by; while their fifteen hundred closely printed pages present the story of Rájpútána in a form little calculated to attract the general reader. The indifference of English publishers to the importance of Tod's labours is a matter both for surprise and regret; though it must be doubted whether the *Annals and Antiquities of Rajasthan*, in the form in which he left it, could ever have become popular. Passages of interest are abundant throughout; but to make one's way through the heavier matter in which they are embedded, demands both time and patience; nor is the task lightened by the author's style, which, though rich and picturesque, is, at times, so loose as to be almost incoherent. The actual annals comprise little more than half the entire work, the remainder consisting of a minute examination into the genealogies of the various Rájpút tribes, an account of their ancient religious beliefs and systems of government, and a lengthy description of the author's own journeyings and experiences. To the student of Indian antiquities these chapters are of undoubted value; but a knowledge of them is by no means essential to an appreciation of the historical narrative.

The present volume is an attempt to rescue from obscurity at least a portion of this once famous work, and to place it before the reader in what, it is hoped, may prove a convenient and attractive form. Mewár, or Udaipúr, with which alone it deals, is, historically, the most important of all the Rájpútána states; for the history of Mewár was, for centuries, the history of Rájpútána, while, at one period, it was almost the history of India. I have endeavoured, as far as possible, to retell the story in Tod's own language, omitting such details as seemed to me to confuse the action, or break the continuity of events, and occasionally introducing, from other portions of the original work, anecdotes and descriptions illustrative of the Rájpúts of Mewár. The more obvious errors of composition have been corrected, and the spelling of proper names has been revised according to the system adopted in the *Imperial Gazetteer of India*. The illustrations have, so far as I know, never been reproduced before. The original drawings were by Colonel Tod's "friend and kinsman," Major Waugh.

C. H. P.

Contents

CONTENTS

List of Illustrations

i.—Introductory

The state of Mewár lies in the south of Rájpútána. In shape and position it resembles a rectangle, placed obliquely, so that the longer sides face north-west and south-east. Let us call it the rectangle ABCD, A and C being the points at the north and south corners, B and D those at the east and west respectively. The side AB separates the state from the British district of Ajmír, the side BC from the territories of Búndi and Málwa, CD from the district of Gujarát, and DA from Sirohi, Godwár, and Márwár or Jodhpúr. The length of the rectangle is roughly 150 miles, its breadth from 80 to 100, and its area is 13,000 square miles. The upper portion is a rich undulating plateau sloping gradually to the north-east, while the lower or south-western portion is almost entirely covered with hills, rocks, and dense jungles. The Arávalli hills extend throughout the entire lengths of the sides AD and DC, increasing in height and width as they approach the point D, where the highest peaks rise more than 4,500 feet above the level of the sea. Mount Abu is a few miles to the west of the point D. Near this spot, and on the eastern side of the hills, rises the principal river of Mewár, the Banás, which, flowing in a direction east by north-east, leaves the state near Deoli on the eastern boundary, and eventually joins the Chambal, of which it is the chief tributary. In the same corner of the rectangle is Udaipúr, the present capital. It is situated in a valley some eighty square miles in extent. Three main passes lead into the valley from the east, while from the west it is almost inaccessible. The ancient capital, Chítor, is situated near the middle point of the side BC. The mountains on this side belong to the Satpúra range, and, though lower than the Arávallis, are equally wild and precipitous, and present a no less effectual barrier against foreign invasion. The whole of this mountainous tract, bordering nearly three sides of the rectangle, is inhabited by the Bhíls and other aboriginal tribes, living in a state of primeval and savage independence. For centuries they acknowledged no paramount power, and paid tribute to none. Their chiefs were men of no small authority and influence, and could, when occasion demanded, muster as many as five thousand bows. The northern portion of the Arávallis averages from six to fifteen miles in breadth, having upwards of one hundred and fifty villages scattered over its valleys. This region is abundantly watered, and not deficient in pasture; there is cultivation enough for all internal wants, though the produce is raised with infinite labour on terraces, as the vine is cultivated in Switzerland and on the Rhine. The valleys abound in variegated quartz and varieties of schistous slate of every hue. The latter is largely used for the roofing of houses and temples, to which, when illumined by the rays of the sun, it gives a most singular appearance. The tin and silver mines of Mewár were, in ancient times, very productive; but, during the domination of the Moguls, political reasons led to the concealment of such sources of wealth, and now the caste of miners is almost extinct.

Copper is still abundant and supplies the currency, while the garnet, the chrysolite, rock crystals, and inferior kinds of the emerald family, are all to be found within the state.

Such are the main features of the country whose story we are about to commence; a country richly endowed by nature, and peopled by one of the noblest races of the east. Within her boundaries Mewár contained all the elements of future greatness; but the very sources of prosperity led to her downfall. Her fertile plains and prosperous cities became a standing temptation to the hoards of hungry invaders who came with monotonous regularity to devastate her fields and batten on her wealth. The Rájpút, with a spirit of constancy and enduring courage to which the history of the world hardly affords a parallel, seized every opportunity to turn upon his oppressors. By his perseverance and valour he wore out entire dynasties of foes. But all was of no avail; fresh supplies were ever pouring in, and dynasty succeeded dynasty, heir to the same remorseless feeling which sanctified murder, legalised spoliation, and deified destruction. For centuries this little state withstood every outrage barbarity could inflict or human nature sustain; until, in the year 1817, her resources broken, her lands alienated, and her people demoralised, she sank exhausted under the protecting arm of Great Britain.

The princes of Mewár are styled Ránas, and are the elder branch of the Súryavánsi or "children of the sun." Amongst his own people the chief of the state is known as *Hindua Suraj*, the "Sun of the Hindus." He is regarded as the legitimate heir to the throne of Ráma, nor has any doubt ever been thrown on the purity of his descent. With the exception of Jaisalmír, Mewár is the only Rájpút state that has outlived eight hundred years of foreign domination; and the Rána of Udaipúr rules to-day over the same territory that his ancestors held when the conqueror from Ghazni first carried his victorious arms across the blue waters[1] of the Indus. The title "Rána" is, comparatively speaking, of modern adoption, and was assumed in consequence of a victory gained over the Prince of Mandor, the original possessor of the title, who surrendered it, together with his life and capital, to the Mewár prince.

The records of the state make Kanáksen, fifty-sixth in descent from the deified Ráma, the founder of the Mewár dynasty, and assign A.D. 145 as the date of his migration from the northern plains of India to the peninsula of Suráshtra. Ráma had two sons, Loh and Cush. Loh, from whom the Rána's family claim descent, is said to have built Lahore, the ancient Lohkót, where his children and his children's children ruled until the days of Kanáksen. By what route Kanáksen made his way from Lohkót to Suráshtra is uncertain. We know, however, that about the middle of the second century he set up his capital at Bírnagara, which place he captured from a chief of the Pramara race, one of the thirty-six royal races of Rájasthán, and that during the next four generations the seat of power was transferred

[1] The river Indus, like the Nile in Egypt, is styled *Niláb*, from níl "blue," and *áb*, "water." *Sindh* is another name for the Indus, a word of Tartar origin, and now applied to the region through which the river flows. In its upper courses the river is termed *âba sin*, "parent stream."

from city to city, and was eventually established at Ballábhipútra, about ten miles north of the present city of Bhownagar. Of the nine princes who here succeeded one another, little but their names is known. We have, in fact, to jump over a period of nearly three hundred years before we again find footing on historical ground. History meets us in A.D. 524, and we learn that in that year Ballábhipútra was overthrown by the Scythians, who, at that period, had begun to abandon the barren steppes of Central Asia for the more fertile plains of Hindustan. "In the west," says an ancient chronicle, "is Súratdes, a country well known. The barbarians invaded it, and conquered the lord of Bhal. All fell in the sack of Ballábhipútra, except the daughter of the Pramara."

The princess referred to in the chronicle was the favourite wife of the Rána. She was not in Ballábhipútra at the time of the siege, having gone to her home to lay an offering at the shrine of Ambabhaváni, the Universal Mother, and to gain thereby a blessing for the child she was shortly to bear. She had already set out on her return journey when news reached her of the calamity which had befallen the city. Stricken with grief, she sought refuge in a mountain cave, and was there delivered of a son. Returning once more to her home, she confided the child to the care of a Brahmini named Camálavati; and having charged her to bring up the young prince as a Brahmin, and to marry him to a Rájpút princess, she mounted the funeral pyre and joined her lord. Camálavati loved the child, and reared him along with her own son. She called him Goha, that is "cave-born," and hence his descendants came to be known as Gohilotes, softened in later times to Gehlotes. The child was a source of perpetual uneasiness to his protectress, and at the age of eleven had become totally unmanageable. He spent his days in the forests in company with the Bhíls, whose habits pleased his daring nature far better than those of the Brahmins. So completely did he win the hearts of these wild people by his strength and his courage, that they determined to make him prince of Idar, and a young Bhíl, cutting his finger, applied the blood as the *tika* of sovereignty to his forehead.

Here again the light of history fails us, and of Goha's subsequent career and of the eight princes who succeeded him on the throne of Idar we know nothing, except that they dwelt in the mountains and that their reigns covered a period of two and a half centuries. The name of the ninth prince was Nagadít. Against him the Bhíls rebelled, having, apparently, grown tired of a foreign rule. Nagadít was slain, and once more the house of Kanáksen was on the verge of extinction. Of the royal house, Bappa, the infant son of Nagadít, alone survived, and, by a strange coincidence, his preservers were the descendants of Camálavati, the Brahmini of Biranagar, who protected and fostered the infant Goha. Bappa was concealed in the hills overlooking Nagda, not ten miles distant from the site of Udaipúr, the future home of his race.

Tradition has preserved many tales of Bappa's infancy. In his boyhood, we are told, he attended the sacred kine, an occupation which was considered honourable even by the "children of the sun." One day, while he was thus engaged, it happened that the daughter of the Solánki chief of Nagda, attended by a band of Rájpút maidens, came to the forest to indulge in the pastime of swinging. Having reached their favourite glade, they discovered that they had come unprovided with a rope, and, chancing to see Bappa, who was grazing his kine in the forest, they called upon him to further their sport. Bappa promised to procure a rope if they would first play a game at marriage. One frolic was as good as another. The scarf of the Solánki princess was fastened to the garment of Bappa, and the Rájpút maidens, joining hands with the pair, formed a ring round an ancient mango tree, and, unwittingly or otherwise, performed the mystic number of evolutions prescribed by the marriage rite. Thus the ceremony, begun in play, ended by being a reality. Not many days after, a suitable offer for the hand of the young princess was received, and the family priest of the would-be bridegroom, whose duty it was to read by the aid of palmistry the fortunes of the bride, made the startling discovery that she was already married. The intelligence, as may well be conceived, caused the greatest consternation. Bappa had little difficulty in swearing his brother shepherds to silence, but a secret shared by so many of the daughters of Eve could hardly remain such long; and before many days had passed the chief of Nagda had a very shrewd suspicion as to who the offender was. Warned of the danger he was in, Bappa sought refuge in the mountains. He was accompanied in his flight by Baleo and Dewa, two faithful Bhíls, who followed the fortunes of their master till he eventually gained the throne of Chítor, and it was

Baleo who, with his own blood, drew the *tika*[1] of sovereignty on the young prince's forehead. The frolic of the youthful shepherd thus proved to be the origin of his greatness, though it burdened him, not only with a wife, but with all the damsels who had taken part in the ceremony, and hence with a numerous issue, whose descendants still ascribe their origin to the prank of Bappa round the old mango tree of Nagda.

At this time, Chítor was ruled by a prince of the Pramara race, known as the Mori, and it was this circumstance which induced Bappa to seek aid in that country; for his mother had been a Pramara princess, and he, therefore, anticipated a favourable reception at the hands of the Mori. Nor was he disappointed. He was welcomed with every sign of friendliness and respect. A suitable estate was conferred upon him, and he was enrolled amongst the *samunts*, or military leaders. The Mori was surrounded by a numerous nobility, holding estates on the tenure of military service. He had never been a popular chief, and the superior regard which he began to display towards Bappa was keenly resented. Indeed, so bitter did the feeling against the Mori become, that when his territory was threatened by a foreign foe, his nobles, instead of obeying the royal summons to arms, threw up their grants, and tauntingly desired him to call upon his favourite.

[1] The descendants of Baleo enjoy the district of Oguna as an hereditary possession. They still claim the privilege of performing the *tika* on the inauguration of a new Rána. The Oguna chief makes an incision in his thumb, and anoints the forehead of the prince with the blood; he then takes him by the arm and seats him on the throne. The Undrí chief, the descendant of Dewa, holds the salver of spices and sacred rice which is also used in making the *tika*.

Bappa readily undertook the conduct of war, and the "barons," though dispossessed of their lands, joined him, for they were ashamed to hold aloof from the fight. He not only inflicted a crushing defeat on the enemy, but by his courage and military skill won the respect and admiration of the refractory nobles. At the close of the campaign, however, the latter refused either to enter Chítor or to yield allegiance to the Mori. Ambassadors were sent to treat with them; but their only reply was that, as they had eaten the salt of the prince, they would forbear their vengeance for twelve months. At the expiration of this period they attacked Chítor, carried the city by assault, and then invited Bappa to become their chief. The gratitude of the Gehlote melted away before the temptation of a crown, and, in the words of the chronicle, "he took Chítor from the Mori, and became himself the *mor* (crown) of the land."

Whether Bappa ruled Chítor well or ill, we have no means of knowing. If tradition is to be believed, he abandoned both his children and his country, carried his arms west to Khorasán, and married new wives from among the "barbarians." He is said to have lived to a patriarchal age, and to have been the father of no less than two hundred and twenty-five children. On his death, the chronicle relates, his subjects quarrelled over the disposal of his remains. The Hindu wished fire to consume them, the "barbarian" to commit them to the earth. But, on raising the pall while the dispute was raging, innumerable flowers of the lotus were found in the place of the remains of mortality.

By a confusion of eras the domestic annals of

Mewár (which bards and chroniclers have followed) give 191 S.V. (era of Vikramáditya), corresponding to A.D. 135, as the date of Bappa's birth. The actual date of this event we now know to be A.D. 713, which, though it curtails by some six hundred years the antiquity of the founder of the state, nevertheless places him in the very dawn of chivalry, when the Carlovingian dynasty flourished in the west, and when Wálid, whose bands planted the green standard on the banks of the Ebro, was commander of the faithful. As has already been stated, the Ránas of Mewár have been in possession of their territories since the time when the armies of Islám first crossed the Indus. It was in the year 95 of the Hejira (A.D. 713) that Muhammad bin Kásim, the general of the caliph, Wálid, conquered Sind, and it has now been established beyond all doubt that Muhammad bin Kásim was the foe whom Bappa repulsed from the walls of Chítor.

ii.—Tartar Invasions

HAVING established the Gehlotes on the throne of Chítor, we must pass over a period of four centuries before we arrive at our next halting-place—the reign of Samársi at the close of the eleventh century, a time fraught with events of importance not only to the state of Mewár but to the whole Hindu race. Thirty-eight princes intervened between Kanáksen and Samársi, and of this long dynastic chain, though the extremities are riveted in the truth, we can point to but few links whose genuineness cannot be called in question. Between Bappa and Samársi we have one such link in the person of Khomán, to whom, for a few moments, we must turn our attention. Khomán ascended the throne in 812, and his deeds are the main theme of the *Khomán Rasa*,[1]

[1] The *Khomán Rasa* traces the genealogy of the Ránas back to Ráma, and deals at length with the Muhammadan irruption in the tenth century, the sack of Chítor by Allah-ud-dín, and the wars of Rána Partáp with Akbar. Of the other poetical chronicles, the *Ráj Vulas*, the *Ráj Ratnakur*, and the *Jai Vulas* are the most important, the two former composed in the reign of Ráj Singh, and the latter in that of Jai Singh. All these chronicles commence with genealogies, and contain accounts of the military exploits of the princes after whom they are called.

The poets were the chief chroniclers of western India; but their magniloquent style and love of romance detract from the historical value of their works; and though they laboured under no actual censorship, there was often a compact between bard and prince which had the double effect of increasing the remuneration of the former and swelling the fame of the latter. Writing for the amusement of a warlike race, the authors disregarded civil matters and the arts and pursuits of peaceful life, and devoted themselves almost exclusively to tales of love and war. But the

the most ancient of the poetic chronicles of Mewár. His most famous achievement was the repulse of the second Muhammadan attack on Chítor led by Mahmún, the son of the renowned Hároun-al-rashíd. Thirty-eight princes aided Khomán with their arms on this occasion, and thus, at the head of all the chivalry of Rájasthán, he not only defended his capital, but led out his forces, engaged and defeated the enemy in the open plain, and took their leader captive. Khomán is said to have fought twenty-four pitched battles, and his name, like that of Cæsar, became a family distinction. At Udaipúr, if you make a false step, or even sneeze, you may still hear the ejaculation "Khomán aid you." When advanced in years, Khomán, by the advice of the Brahmins, resigned his throne to his son, but again resumed it, slaying his advisers, and execrating the whole Brahmin caste, which he almost exterminated from his dominions. The fifteen princes who came between him and Samársi may be dismissed with the words in which Gibbon refers to the Guelphs during a

loss to posterity on this latter account is perhaps not so great as it would appear to be; for though admitted to a knowledge of the secret springs which worked the administrative machinery, the bards participated too deeply in the intrigues and levities of the court to be impartial judges of the actions of either their chief or his ministers.

Nevertheless, though open to these objections, the works of the bards narrate many interesting facts and incidents, and throw much valuable light on religious opinion and the manners and habits of the people. Nor were their writers afraid to utter, at times, truths extremely unpalatable to their royal patrons. When offended, or actuated by virtuous indignation against what they deemed acts of immorality, they were fearless of consequences, and woe to the individual who provoked them. Many a resolution sank under the lash of their satire, and many a name that might otherwise have escaped notoriety was condemned by the same agency to eternal ridicule. The poison of the bard was more dreaded by the Rájpút than the steel of his foe.

similar period of obscurity: "It may be supposed that they were illiterate and valiant; that they plundered in their youth, and raised churches in their old age; that they were fond of arms, horses, and hunting"; and, we may add, that they indulged in bickering with their vassals within when not harassed by an enemy without.

When Samársi ascended the throne of Chítor, violent and implacable feuds were raging in Rájpútána. A complete analysis of the political situation would be a weary, if not an impossible, task. It is necessary, however, to understand the main points at issue; for it was the confusion following these feuds which paved the way for the victorious armies of Islám.

Every Rájpút, no matter to which of the thirty-six royal tribes he may belong, is either of the solar, the lunar, or the agnicular race. In the first case he traces his origin through Ráma to the sun, in the second case through Krishna to the moon, and in the third case to Agni, the Fire God. The Gehlotes, as we have already stated, are of the solar race, and, being descended from the elder son of Ráma, are universally acknowledged to be the first of the royal tribes. The Rahtors—a tribe of hardly less importance—also claim to be of this race; but the purity of their descent is open to question. Of the lunar race, the most important tribes are the Tuárs and the Bhattis; and of the last, the Chohans, the Pramaras, and the Solánkis.

Until 1164 a Tuár dynasty reigned at Delhi, the most powerful of all the Rájpút principalities. Anangpál, the last of the dynasty, is now generally admitted to have been a lineal descendant of Yudhistara, who founded Indraprastha, the ancient

Delhi, in B.C. 1030. He therefore presents the extraordinary phenomenon of a prince occupying a throne established by a direct ancestor of his own two thousand two hundred and fifty years before. Anangpál, having no male issue, abdicated in favour of Prithvi Ráj, the son of the Chohan prince of Ajmír, to whom, in return for service rendered, he had given one of his daughters in marriage. Now, the Rahtor prince of Kanouj had also married a daughter of the Tuár, by whom he had a son, Jaichand; and when Prithvi Ráj was proclaimed the chief of Delhi, Jaichand not only refused to acknowledge his supremacy, but at once set forth his own claims to the throne. Thus originated the rivalry between the Chohans and the Rahtors, which ultimately led to the destruction of both.

To accomplish the downfall of his rival, Jaichand had recourse to the dangerous expedient of soliciting aid from the Tartar of Ghazni. In this emergency Prithvi Ráj sent an embassy to Samársi, to whom, but a short time before, he had given his sister in marriage, urging him to espouse his cause. Samársi at once promised his assistance, not only because he was the Tuár's brother-in-law, but because he was disgusted at the course which Jaichand had adopted in making an alliance with the "barbarian." He immediately proceeded to Delhi, and it was decided that Prithvi Ráj should give battle to the Rahtor, while Samársi marched towards Ghazni to intercept the forces of Shaháb-ud-dín. Samársi fought several actions, and was at length joined by Prithvi Ráj, who had in the meantime subdued the Rahtors. United they fell upon and completely routed the invaders, and took their leader captive.

Not many years later Samársi was again called upon to aid Delhi in repelling a Tartar attack, led this time by Shaháb-ud-dín in person. Foreseeing a long campaign, he appointed his son regent before his departure. His arrival at Delhi was hailed with shouts of joy, Prithvi Ráj and his whole court advancing seven miles to meet him. By the bards Samársi is represented as the Ulysses of the host—cool and skilful in the fight, prudent and eloquent in council, beloved by his own nobles, and reverenced by the vassals of the Chohan. On the line of march no augur could better explain the omens, none in the field better dress the squadrons for battle, none guide his steed or use his lance with more address. His tent is the principal resort of the leaders after the march or during the intervals of battle.

In the bloody encounter which ensued the deeds of prowess which the brave Gehlote performed are still sung by the bards of Mewár. The jealous and revengeful nature of Jaichand rendered him an indifferent spectator of a contest that was fraught with disaster for himself and his country. Gehlotes and Chohans fought as only Rájpúts could fight. But all was in vain. On the last of three days desperate fighting Samársi was slain, together with 1,300 of his household troops. His beloved wife, Pritha, was awaiting the issue at Delhi. On hearing the fatal intelligence—her husband killed, her brother a captive, and all the chivalry of Delhi and Chítor "asleep on the banks of the Caggar,"[1]—she per-

[1] The Caggar is said to have been absorbed into the desert during the reign of Rána Hamír. It rose in the Sewálik hills, flowed westward through Hissár, and eventually emptied itself into the Indus a few miles to the south of Uch.

formed, like a true Rájpútni, the great atonement, and joined her lord through the flame. Shaháb-ud-dín marched on Delhi, which he carried by storm. Kanouj fell not long after, and the traitor to his nation met his fate in the waters of the Ganges. Scenes of devastation, plunder, and massacre followed. Every road in Rájasthán ran with the blood of the spoiled and the spoiler. Whole tribes were swept away, and their names are the only memento of their former existence and celebrity.

Kurna succeeded Samársi. His reign presents few features of interest, and the same may be said of the ten princes who followed him. Of these, Rahup alone is worthy of mention. He it was who, shortly after his accession in 1201, conquered the Rána of Mandor, and annexed both his territory and his title. He also built the town of Sesoda, which gave rise to the appellation "Sesodia," by which from this time forward the Rájpúts of Mewár are known. He reigned for nearly forty years, and did much to restore the fallen fortunes of the state. Of the remaining nine, six fell on the field of battle in chivalrous attempts to redeem the sacred Gya from pollution at the hands of the "barbarian," while confusion and strife within and without characterised the reigns of each one of them. The dust of the centuries lies thick upon them; let us leave it undisturbed, and pass on to the next great event in the annals of the state—an event which partakes more of the character of romance than history, though the facts are undoubted.

Of all the events described in the annals of Mewár, none are more memorable than those which fell in the reign of Lakumsi, when Chítor, the repository of all that was precious of the arts of India, was stormed, sacked, and desecrated with remorseless barbarity by the Pathán emperor Allah-ud-dín. Lakumsi was a minor when he ascended the *gadi* in 1274, and Bhímsi, his uncle, acted as regent and protector. Bhímsi had married a Chohan princess, by name Pudmani, who was of surpassing beauty. Indeed, if her charms were inferior to those of the heroine of Troy, they were not less fatal in their consequences; for, according to the bard chroniclers, it was the desire to possess this peerless princess, rather than the acquisition of military fame, which prompted Allah-ud-dín to attack Chítor.

The city was strongly fortified and bravely defended, and after a long and fruitless siege, Allah-ud-dín, who made no attempt to disguise the object of his attack, offered to withdraw his forces if his demand for the surrender of Pudmani were satisfied. At length, when negotiations and force had alike proved unavailing, the cunning Pathán restricted his demands to a mere sight of this extraordinary beauty, and even acceded to the proposal that he should see her through the medium of mirrors. Relying on the faith of the Rájpút, he entered Chítor unguarded, and, having gratified his wish, took his departure. Bhímsi, not to be outdone in confidence, accompanied the king to the foot of the fortress. This was the opportunity on which Allah-ud-dín had calculated, and for which he had risked his own safety. His ambush was ready. Bhímsi was made a prisoner, hurried away to the Tartar camp, and the surrender of Pudmani was announced as the price of his liberty.

Dismay reigned in Chítor when this fatal mishap became known. Pudmani, armed with the means of securing herself against dishonour, was about to proceed to the Tartar camp, when her uncle Gorah and his nephew Bádal suggested a plan for the liberation of Bhímsi by which neither her life nor her fair name would be endangered. A message was sent to Allah-ud-dín that, on the day that he withdrew from his trenches, the princess would be sent to his tents; but in a manner befitting her high station, and accompanied by her female relations and handmaids, while stringent orders were to be issued by the Emperor for the preservation of their privacy. The conditions were accepted; and, on the day appointed, no less than seven hundred litters proceeded to the royal camp. Each litter was occupied by one of the bravest warriors of Chítor, and was borne by six armed soldiers disguised as bearers. Allah-ud-dín had no suspicion of the ruse, and none cried "equo ne credite." The Emperor's tents were surrounded by high canvas screens, and when the litters had been deposited within the enclosure, half an hour was granted for a parting interview between Bhímsi and his bride. The time had all but expired, and Allah-ud-dín was about to give orders for the termination of the interview, when the Rájpúts threw off their disguise. In the confusion which ensued, Bhímsi made his escape from the enclosure, and, mounting a horse which had been placed in readiness for him, made for the fortress. His gallant rescuers covered his retreat until they perished to a man. For a moment only their devotion checked the pursuit. But it was enough; and Bhímsi galloped into Chítor with the Tartar host at his very heels.

In the assault which followed, the Rájpúts, headed

by Gorah and Bádal, displayed the utmost bravery. Gorah was slain, and with him nearly every warrior of note in Chítor. But so terrible was the havoc they made in the ranks of the enemy, that Allah-ud-dín was forced to retire, and to abandon, though only for a time, his cherished enterprise. The *Khomán Rasa* contains a vivid description of the manner in which the wife of Gorah received the intelligence of her husband's death. The details are, doubtless, imaginary; but that they are consistent with the truth we can well believe. Summoning Bádal, who, though but a stripling, had been severely wounded in the fight, she desired him to relate how her lord had conducted himself. "He was the reaper," the youth replied, "of the harvest of battle. On the gory bed of honour he spread a carpet of the slain. A barbarian prince his pillow he laid him down, and he sleeps surrounded by the foe." Again she said: "Tell me, Bádal, how did my love behave?" "O mother," said the lad, "how further describe his deeds, when he left no foe to dread or admire him?" She smiled farewell to the boy, and adding, "my lord will chide my delay," sprang into the flames.

Several years elapsed, and Lakumsi had assumed the control of the state, before Allah-ud-dín found himself strong enough to renew his attack on Chítor. The history of this second siege is copiously interwoven with legends. The latter, however, do not obscure the facts, but merely fill up gaps, or account for circumstances for which history offers no explanation. From the outset, there seems to have been little chance of saving the city. Allah-ud-dín had an overwhelming force at his disposal, and every day the vigour of his assaults increased. One night, when the Rána lay stretched on his pallet, pondering as to how he might preserve at least one of his twelve sons from the destruction which he knew to be inevitable, he heard a voice saying, "*main bhúka hún*" (I am hungry), and raising his eyes he saw, by the dim glare of the lamp, advancing between the granite columns, the majestic form of the guardian goddess of Chítor. "Not satiated," exclaimed the Rána, "though eight thousand of my kin were late an offering to thee?" "I must have regal victims," was the inexorable reply, "and if twelve who wear the diadem bleed not for Chítor, the land will pass from the line."

On the morn he convened a council of his chiefs, to whom he revealed the vision of the night, which they treated as the dream of a disordered fancy. He commanded their attendance at midnight, when again the form appeared, and repeated the terms on which alone she would remain amongst them. "Though thousands of barbarians strew the earth, what are they to me? On each day enthrone a prince. Let the *kirnia*, the *chhatra*, and the *chamara*[1] proclaim his sovereignty, and for three days let his decrees be supreme: on the fourth let him meet the foe and his fate." Whether we have merely the fiction of the poet, or whether the scene was got up to animate the spirit of resistance, matters little; it is consistent with the belief of the tribe; and the gage, whether it originated with the goddess or with the Rána, was fully accepted, and fully redeemed.

[1] These are the insignia of royalty. The *kirnia* is a parasol, from *kiran*, a ray; the *chhatra* is the umbrella, always red; the *chamara*, the flowing tail of the wild ox, set in a gold handle, and used to drive away the flies.

Photo. by] [*Donald Macbeth, London*

THE PALACE OF BHÍMSI AND PUDMANI.

p. 20

On the conditions being known, a generous contention arose amongst the brave brothers as to who should be the first victim to avert the denunciation. Arsi urged his priority of birth ; he was proclaimed, the umbrella waved over his head, and on the fourth day he surrendered his short-lived honours and his life. Ajaisi, the next in birth, demanded to follow; but he was the favourite son of his father, and at the latter's request he consented to let his brothers precede him. Eleven victims had fallen in turn, and a contest then arose between the Rána and his surviving son. But the father prevailed, and Ajaisi, in obedience to his commands, with a small band of followers, passed safely through the enemy's lines, and took refuge in Kailwára.

The Rána, satisfied that his line was not extinct, prepared to follow his brave sons. But another awful sacrifice, the terrible *johur*, was to precede this last act of self-devotion. The funeral pyre was lighted in the "great subterranean retreat," in chambers impervious to the light of day, and thither the defenders of Chítor watched their wives and daughters pass in procession, to the number of several thousands. The fair Pudmani closed the throng, and when all had entered the cavern, the doors were shut upon them, and they were left to find security from dishonour in the devouring element. Then the Rána ordered the gates of Chítor to be thrown open, and, calling his clans around him, descended to the plain, where he, and every man with him, hurled himself against the foe, and slew until he was himself slain.

After the Tartar irruption, Rájpútána resembled a country swept by a tornado ; her citadels and temples in ruins, her villages abandoned, her fields devastated. Of the dynasties that were overthrown, some, like Chítor, Jaisalmír, and Búndi, were destined to raise their heads again. Others perished utterly. The Rahtors of Márwár, and the Cutchwáhas of Ambar were yet in a state of insignificance. But the Pramaras, the Solánkis, indeed every branch of the Agnicular race, ceased from that time to have any political existence. Allah-ud-dín remained some days in Chítor, admiring the greatness of his conquest; and having committed every act of barbarity and vandalism which a bigoted zeal could suggest, he handed over the city in charge to Maldeo, the Hindu chief of Jhálawár, whom he had conquered and enrolled among his vassals.

This was the first *saca* of Chítor. Altogether the annals reckon three and a half, the assault after the escape of Bhímsi being counted as the half; for though the city was not captured, the best and bravest were cut off (*saca*).[1] Amongst the Rájpúts, all grand battles attended with great slaughter were termed *saca*. "By the sin of the sack of Chítor," *Chítor ká saca ká páp*, is the most solemn form of adjuration a Rájpút can make use of.

[1] The Arabic word *saca* signifies a sudden fall or blow, particularly the striking of lightning.

iii.—Recovery of Chítor

THE survivor of Chítor, Rána Ajaisi, was now in security at Kailwára, a town in the heart of the Arávalli mountains, and at the highest point of one of the most extensive valleys of the range. Here he gradually collected about him the remnants of the clans of Mewár. It was the last behest of his father that when he attained "one hundred years" (a figurative expression for dying), the son of Arsi, the elder brother, should succeed him. This injunction, from the deficiency of noble qualities in his own sons, he readily fulfilled. Hamír was the name of the son of Arsi, at this time a lad of twelve.

Ajaisi, besides being an exile from his capital, had to contend with the chieftains of the mountains, amongst whom the most formidable was Munja, who had on a former occasion raided the Shero Nalla, the valley where the Rána was now concealed, and had wounded him on the head with a spear. Sajunsi and Ajunsi, his own sons, though fourteen and fifteen years old, an age at which a Rájpút ought to indicate his future character, proved of little aid in the emergency. Hamír, however, accepted the feud against Munja, and set out in search of him, promising to return successful or not at all. In a few days he was seen entering the pass of Kailwára with Munja's head at his saddle-bow. Modestly placing the trophy at his uncle's feet, he exclaimed: "Recognise the head of your foe." This decided the fate of the sons of Ajaisi, one of whom died at Kailwára, and the other, Sajunsi, departed for the Dekhan, where his issue rose to fame; for he was the ancestor of Siváji, the founder of the Satára throne, and his lineage is given in the chronicles of Mewár.

Hamír succeeded in 1301, and had sixty-four years granted him to redeem his country from the ruin which had befallen it. The day on which he assumed the ensigns of rule, he displayed in the *tíka-dour* an earnest of his future energy. He made a rapid inroad into the heart of Balaitcha, the country of his late enemy, Munja, and captured its principal stronghold, a circumstance which his followers regarded as a sure omen of his future greatness. The *tíka-dour* signifies the foray of inauguration. It is a custom that has been observed from time immemorial, and is still maintained where any semblance of hostility affords opportunity for its practice. On the morning of the installation, having received the *tíka* of sovereignty, the prince at the head of his retainers makes a foray into the territory of any one with whom he may have a feud, or with whom he may be indifferent as to exciting one; he captures a stronghold or plunders a town, and returns with the trophies. If amity should prevail all around, a mock representation of the custom takes place.

When Ajaisi died, Maldeo, with the imperial forces, was still holding Chítor; but he was not left in undisturbed possession. Hamír desolated the plains, and left to his enemy only the fortified towns which could be occupied with safety. He commanded all who owned his sovereignty either to quit their abodes and retire with their families to the shelter of the hills on the eastern and western frontiers, or be reckoned amongst his enemies. The roads were rendered impassable from his bands, to whom the intricate defiles of the hills offered a means of retreat which baffled all pursuit. He made Kailwára his residence, which became the chief refuge of the emigrants from the plains. The town was admirably situated, being approached by narrow defiles, while a steep pass led over the mountains to a still more inaccessible retreat, where at a later time the fortress of Komulmír was built, well-watered and wooded, and with excellent pasturage. This tract, above 50 miles in breadth, is 1,200 feet above the level of the plain and 3,000 above the sea, with a considerable quantity of arable land, and free communication to the west by which supplies could be procured from Márwár or Gujarát, as well as from the principal Bhíl tracts, to whose inhabitants more than one Rána of Mewár was indebted for assistance in the hour of need. The elevated plateau of the eastern frontier contained places of almost equal security; but Allah-ud-dín traversed these in person, devastating as he went.

Such was the state of Mewár; its fortresses occupied by the foe, cultivation and peaceful pursuits abandoned in consequence of the persevering hostility of Hamír, when Maldeo endeavoured to conciliate his persecutor by offering him in marriage the hand of a Hindu princess. Contrary to the wishes of his advisers, Hamír directed that "the cocoa-nut should be retained,"[1] coolly remarking

[1] A cocoa-nut is always sent with such a proposal. Its return signifies that the alliance is declined, and is usually regarded as an insult by the sender.

on the dangers pointed out, "my feet shall at least ascend the rocky steps trodden by my ancestors." It was stipulated that only five hundred horse should form his suite, and thus accompanied, he set out for Chítor.

On his approach, the five sons of Maldeo advanced to meet him, but on the portal of the city no *torun* was suspended. He, however, accepted the unsatisfactory reply to his remark on its omission, and ascended for the first time the ramp of Chítor. The *torun* is the symbol of marriage, and its absence would be regarded as an omen of the worst description. It consists of three wooden bars, fastened together in the form of an equilateral triangle, and surmounted by the image of a peacock. This emblem is suspended either from the gate of the city, or the portal of the bride. The bridegroom on horseback, lance in hand, proceeds to break the *torun*, which is defended by the damsels of the bride, who, from the parapet, assail him with missiles of various kinds, and especially with a red powder made from the flower of the *palása*, at the same time singing songs fitted to the occasion. At length the *torun* is broken amidst the shouts of the bridegroom's retainers, when the fair defenders retire.

Hamír was received in the ancient halls of his ancestors by Maldeo, his son Banbír, and other chiefs. The bride was led forth and presented by her father, but without any of the solemnities customary on such occasions; "the knot of their garments was tied, their hands united," and thus they were left. It was the princess herself who revealed to Hamír the significance of the barren ceremonial. He had married a widow! His wrath at the insult thus offered to him was great; but when he learnt that his bride had been married in infancy, that the bridegroom died shortly afterwards, and that she could not even recollect his face, he grew calmer; and as he listened to her vows of fidelity, and to a scheme which she revealed to him for the recovery of Chítor, he became more than reconciled to his fate. It is a privilege possessed by a bridegroom to have one specific favour complied with as a part of the marriage dower, and Hamír was instructed by his bride to ask for the services of Jal, one of the civil officers of Chítor, and, with his bride thus obtained, and the retainer whose talents remained for trial, he made his way back to Kailwára.

Kaitsi was the fruit of this marriage, and a few months after his birth, the princess, feigning some defect in the household gods of Kailwára, obtained from her parents permission to bring the child to Chítor and place him before the shrine of his ancestors. The time had been well chosen, for Maldeo, with a large portion of his troops, was absent on a military expedition. Escorted by a party from Chítor, she entered the city, and, through the medium of Jal, succeeded in gaining over the troops that were left. Hamír was at hand; and a few hours later he was master of the fortress. Maldeo, on his return, was met with a "salute of arabas,"[1] and, his force being too weak to attempt an assault, he carried the news of his loss to King Mahmúd, who had succeeded Allah-ud-dín on the throne of Delhi. The "standard of the sun" once more shone refulgent from the walls of Chítor, and the adherents

[1] A kind of arquebus.

of Hamír returned from the hills to their ancient abodes.

But it was not long before Mahmúd advanced to the recovery of his lost possession. Fortunately for Mewar, he directed his march by way of the eastern plateau, where the intricacies of the country robbed him of all the advantage his superior numbers would have given him had he entered by the plains of the north. Hamír, supported by every chief in Mewár, marched to meet him. The armies met at Singoli, and after a bloody encounter Mahmúd was defeated and made prisoner. He was confined for three months in Chítor, and only released when he had agreed to surrender Ajmír, Rinthambúr, an important fortress in the south-east corner of the state, and Nágor, and to pay an indemnity of six lakhs of rupees and a hundred elephants.

Banbír, the son of Maldeo, offered to serve Hamír, and was given a post of honour and an estate for his maintenance. As he made the grant, Hamír said: "Eat, serve, and be faithful. Remember that you are no longer the servant of a Toork, but of a Hindu of your own faith." Banbír shortly after carried by assault the ancient fortress of Bhainsror on the Chambal, which was incorporated with Mewár, whose boundaries were now more widely extended than they had ever been before. Hamír was the sole Hindu prince of power left in India; all the ancient dynasties were crushed, and the ancestors of the present rulers of Márwár and Jaipúr paid him homage and obeyed his summons, as did the princes of Búndi, Gwalior, Chandéri, Raisen, and Abu. He died full of years, leaving a name still honoured in Mewár, as one of the wisest and most gallant of her princes, and bequeathing a well-established and extensive power to his son.

During the two centuries which followed the recovery of the capital, the strength and solidity of the power of Mewár were greater than at any other period of her history. Though almost surrounded by Muhammadan kingdoms, Delhi in the north, Málwa in the south, and Gujarát in the west, she successfully opposed them all. The dynasty in possession, for the time being, of the imperial throne, Tughlak, Khilji, or Lodi, courted the favour of the Ránas, whose power was so consolidated that they were able not only to repel the invader, but to carry their victorious arms abroad to Suráshtra in the west, and in the north to the very walls of the Mogul capital. Besides a long repose, their subjects must have enjoyed high prosperity during this epoch, if we may judge from the magnificence of their public works, when a single triumphal column cost the income of a kingdom to erect. The Ránas were invariably patrons of the arts, more especially of architecture, and every year saw the capital enriched with new and costly monuments. That it was possible to set aside vast sums for works of this nature, and at the same time to provide adequate means for the defence of her constantly-increasing territories, shows how very considerable the revenues of the state had become. The annual military expenditure must have been enormous; for it included not only the maintenance of a large standing army, consisting almost entirely of cavalry, but the upkeep and garrisoning of no less than eighty-four fortresses.

Khaitsi succeeded in 1365. He still further

extended his boundaries, adding to his dominions Jahájpúr, Patan, and the whole district of Chappan, and he gained a signal victory over the monarch of Delhi at Bakrole. Unhappily, his life terminated in a family broil with the vassal chief of Banoda, whose daughter he was about to espouse. His place was taken by Lakha Rána, whose first act was the subjugation of the mountainous region known as Merwára, embracing the upper portion of the Arávalli range, forming the north-western boundary of the state. But an event of much greater importance, and which most powerfully tended to the prosperity of the country, was the discovery of tin and silver mines in the newly-acquired district of Chappan. Lakha was the first to work them, and the profit resulting therefrom was expended on the excavation of reservoirs, the erection of strongholds, and the rebuilding of the temples and palaces demolished by Allah-ud-dín. A portion of his own palace yet exists, in the same style of architecture as the more ancient one, the abode of the fair Pudmani. A temple which he built, and dedicated to the creator, Bramha, an enormous and costly fabric, is also in existence; being the shrine of "the One," and consequently containing no idol, it may thus have escaped the ruthless fury of the invaders.

Lakha encountered the emperor Muhammad Shah Lodi, and on one occasion defeated an imperial army near Bednor, the fortress erected for the defence of the recently-subdued Merwára tract. He lived to an advanced age, and gave up his life in an attempt to expel the "barbarian" from the holy city, Gya. Such an act of devotion was by no means uncommon among the early princes of Rájasthán, many of

Photo by Donald Macbeth, London

PILLAR OF VICTORY AT CHITOR.

[p. 30

whom, at the approach of old age, sought to make their peace with heaven "for the sins inevitably committed by one who wields a sceptre" by embarking on the holy war, in which to meet death was to secure beatitude in the next world, and exemption from second birth.

iv.—Chonda and Khúmbho

THOUGH lacking the refinements of the more cultured nations of the west, there was one respect in which the Rájpút could vie with the most civilised men of any age or clime, namely, in his devotion to the fair sex. Like the ancient German or Scandinavian, he consulted his wife in every transaction; from her ordinary actions he drew the omen of success, and he appended to her name the epithet *devi*, or godlike. In spite of her incarceration, the influence of the Rájpútni in public as well as domestic affairs was often far more powerful than that of her husband. *C'est aux hommes à faire des grandes choses, c'est aux femmes à les inspirer*, is a maxim to which no Rájpút cavalier would have refused to subscribe. He knew there was no retreat into which the report of a gallant exploit would not penetrate, and set fair hearts in motion to be the object of his search; and he was ready to engage in the most desperate enterprise to protect the honour, or win the regard of the lady of his choice. Nothing fired his resentment more speedily than an offence against female delicacy, and there are many instances in the history of Rájasthán when a ribald jest was sufficient to cause a feud which generations of bloodshed could not extinguish.

But however exalted the respect of the Rájpút for the fair sex, he nevertheless held that

> Nothing lovelier can be found
> In woman, than to study household good;

and inattention to domestic duties was a crime not to be overlooked. On one occasion, during the most tempestuous period of the history of Mewár, the Rána had bestowed a daughter on a foreign chieftain, to whom he had made a grant of the district of Sádri; and the royal bride showed a disposition to resent the control of her less exalted lord and master. To the courteous request, "Ranáwatji, fill me a cup of water," he received a contemptuous refusal, with the remark that the daughter of a hundred kings would not become cup-bearer to the chieftain of Sádri. "Very well," replied the plain soldier, "you may return to your father's house, if you can be of no use in mine." A messenger was instantly sent to the court, and the incident, with every aggravation, was reported. The princess followed on the heels of her messenger, and a summons soon arrived for the Sádri chief to attend his sovereign at the capital. He obeyed; and arrived in time to give his explanation just as the Rána was proceeding to hold a full court. As usual, the Sádri chief was placed on his sovereign's right hand, and when the court broke up, the heir-apparent of Mewár, at a preconcerted sign, stood at the edge of the carpet, performing the menial office of holding the slippers of the chief. Shocked at such a mark of extreme respect, he stammered forth some words of homage, his unworthiness, etc., to which the Rána replied, "As my son-in-law, no distinction too great can be conferred: take home your wife, she will never again refuse you a cup of water."

To illustrate the respect and deference to which the Rájpútni was accustomed we will give another short anecdote. The celebrated Rája Jai Singh of

Ambar had espoused a princess of Haravati, whose manners and garb, accordant with the simplicity of that provincial capital, subjected her to the *badinage* of the more advanced court of Ambar, whose ladies had exchanged their national dress for that of the imperial court at Delhi. One day, when alone with his bride, the prince began playfully to contrast the sweeping *jupe* of Kotah with the more scanty robe of the belles of his own capital, and, taking up a pair of scissors, said he would reduce it to an equality with the latter. Offended at such levity, she seized his sword, and, assuming a threatening attitude, said that in the house to which she had the honour to belong, they were not habituated to jests of such a nature; that mutual respect was the guardian, not only of happiness but of virtue; and she assured him, that if he ever again so insulted her, he would find that the daughter of Kotah could use a sword more effectively than the prince of Ambar the scissors, adding, that she would prevent any further scion of her house from being subjected to similar disrespect, by declaring such intermarriages *tilac*, or forbidden, which interdict yet exists.

It was a jest of an equally harmless description which robbed Chonda, the eldest son of Lakha, of his throne, and which, in its consequences, proved more disastrous to the fortunes of Mewár than the armies of the Moguls. Lakha Rána was advanced in years, his sons and grandsons established in suitable domains, when "the cocoa-nut came" from Rinmal, prince of Mandor, to affiance his daughter with the heir of Mewár. When the embassy was announced, Chonda was absent, and the old chief was seated in his chair of state, surrounded by his court. He received the messenger of Hymen courteously, and observed that Chonda would soon return and take the gage; "for," added he, drawing his fingers over his mustachios, "I don't suppose you send such playthings to an old greybeard like me." This little sally was, of course, applauded and repeated, and Chonda, offended at delicacy being sacrificed to wit, declined to accept the symbol which his father had, even in jest, supposed might be intended for himself. The old Rána was greatly incensed at his son's obstinacy, and, as the cocoa-nut could not be returned without gross insult to Rinmal, he decided to accept it himself. He made Chonda swear that, in the event of his having a son, he would renounce his birthright, and be to the child but "the first of his Rájpúts"; and Chonda swore by Eklinga, the presiding deity of the Sesodias, to fulfil his father's wishes.

Within a year of his marriage, a son, Mokul, was born, and, to ensure his peaceful succession, the Rána, before setting out on his crusade to Gya, caused the ceremony of his installation to be performed. Chonda was the first to do homage and swear fidelity to the future sovereign, only reserving for himself, as the recompense for his renunciation, the first place in the councils, and stipulating that in all grants to the vassals of the crown his own symbol, the lance,[1]

[1] The martial Rájpúts are not strangers to armorial bearings. The great banner of Mewár exhibits a golden sun on a crimson field; those of the chiefs bear a dagger. Ambar displays the *panchranga*, or five-coloured flag. The lion rampant on an argent field was the emblem of Chandéri. The peacock was also a favourite emblem, and a peacock's feather often adorned the turban of a Rájpút warrior. These emblems had a religious significance amongst the Rájpúts, and were adopted from their

should be superadded to the signature of the chief, a practice which obtains to the present day.

The sacrifice of Chonda to offended delicacy was great; for besides being brave, frank, and a skilled soldier, he possessed all the qualities requisite for a ruler; and after his father's departure and death, he conducted the public affairs of the state with ability and success. But the queen-mother, the natural guardian of her infant's rights, felt umbrage and discontent at her loss of power, forgetting that, but for Chonda, she would never have been mother to the Rána of Mewár. She watched with a jealous eye all his proceedings, and made no attempt to conceal her suspicions that he was aiming at absolute sovereignty, and that if he did not assume the title of Rána, he would reduce it to an empty name. Chonda, knowing the purity of his own motives, for some time made allowances for maternal solicitude; but his position soon became unendurable, and he threw up the reins of government in disgust. Bidding his successor look well to the rights of the Sesodias, he retired to the court of Mándu, where he was received with distinction, and the district of Hallár was assigned to him by the prince.

His departure was the signal for an influx of the kindred of the queen, amongst whom were her brother Joda (who afterwards gave his name to Jodhpúr), and her father, the old Rao Rinmal. It was soon seen that Chonda's parting words were no idle warning, and the queen-mother found that, instead of safe-

mythology. A famous Khíchí leader, Jai Singh never went to battle without the god of his house at his saddle bow. "Victory to Bajrang" was his signal for the charge so dreaded by the Mahráttas, and often was the deity sprinkled with his blood and that of his foe.

guarding her own position and her son's interests, she had jeopardised both. With his grandson on his knee, the old Rao would sit on the throne of Mewár, and when the boy quitted him for play, the royal ensigns continued to wave over his head. This was more than the Sesodia nurse could bear, and one day, bursting with indignation, she demanded of the queen if her kin was to defraud her own child of his inheritance. Thoroughly alarmed, the queen addressed a remonstrance to her father, the only reply to which was a hint threatening the life of her offspring. Her fears were soon increased by the assassination of Raghudeva, Chonda's brother, a prince beloved by the Sesodias for his virtues and manly courage.

In this extremity, the queen-mother turned her thoughts to Chonda, and she contrived to apprise him of the danger which threatened his race. The latter, on his departure from Chítor, had been accompanied by 200 huntsmen, whose ancestors had served the chiefs of Mewár from ancient times. On the pretext of visiting their families, whom they had left behind, these men gained admission to the city, and succeeded in getting themselves enrolled among the keepers of the gates. The queen-mother was counselled to cause the young prince to descend daily with a numerous retinue to give feasts to the surrounding villages, and not to fail, on the "festival of lamps," to hold the feast at Gosúnda.

The instructions were carefully attended to. The day arrived; the feast was held at Gosúnda; but night began to close in, and no Chonda appeared. With heavy hearts the nurse, the *purohit*, or family priest, and others in the secret, moved homeward. They had reached the eminence known as Chítori, when forty horsemen passed them at a gallop, and at their head Chonda in disguise, who by a secret sign paid homage as he passed to his younger brother and sovereign. The band reached the upper gate unchecked, and when challenged said that they were neighbouring chieftains who, hearing of the feast at Gosúnda, had the honour to escort the young prince home. The story obtained credit; but the main body, of which this was but the advance, presently coming up, the treachery was apparent. Chonda unsheathed his sword, and, at his well-known shout, his hunters were speedily in action. The gates were flung open, the guards cut to pieces, and in a few moments every Rahtor had been killed or hunted out of the city.

The end of Rao Rinmal was more ludicrous than tragical. When the gates were rushed, he was in his palace, half intoxicated with wine, and dallying with a Sesodia maiden whom force had compelled to his side. The drunken old chief was no match for the lithe Rájpútni, who, hearing the tumult without, dexterously bound him to his bed with his own Márwári turban; and, before his dazed senses could realise what was taking place, the messengers of fate were at the door of his apartment. Wild with rage, he struggled to extricate himself, and by some tortuosity of movement got upon his legs, his pallet at his back like a shell. With no arms but a brass vessel of ablution, he levelled to the ground more than one of his assailants, before a ball from a matchlock extended him on the floor of his palace.

But Chonda's revenge was not yet satisfied. He pursued Rao Joda who, though he managed to make good his escape, was obliged to leave Mandor to its fate. This city Chonda entered by surprise and captured without difficulty. It was held bv his two sons, whom he left in possession, for a period of twelve years, at the end of which time, Joda, with the assistance of the chieftains of Mewoh and Pábúji, succeeded in recovering his capital. The elder son of Chonda with many adherents was slain; and the younger, deserted by the subjects of Mandor, trusted to the swiftness of his horse to escape, but was overtaken, and killed on the borders of Godwár. Thus Joda, in his turn, was avenged; but "the fued was not balanced." Two sons of Chítor had fallen for one chief of Mandor. But wisely reflecting on the original aggression, and on the superior power of Mewár, Joda sued for peace, and to quench the feud, agreed that the spot where Chonda's younger son fell should be the future barrier of the two states. The entire province of Godwár was comprehended in this cession, and remained in the possession of the Ránas for more than three centuries. Chonda's name is one of the most famous in the annals of Mewár, and he was the founder of the famous clan called after him the Chondáwats, who played so prominent a part in the later history of the state.

Mokul, who obtained the throne by Chonda's surrender of his birthright, succeeded in 1398, and reigned not unworthily for twenty years. He took possession of Sámbur and its salt lakes, and otherwise strengthened and extended his territories, which the distracted state of the country, consequent on Timúr's invasion, rendered a matter of little difficulty.

He was murdered by his uncles, the natural brothers of his father, who considered themselves affronted by a supposed allusion, on the part of the prince, to the irregularity of their origin. He was followed by his son Khúmbho in 1419, under whom Mewár reached the zenith of her prosperity.

A hundred years had elapsed since Allah-ud-dín had trampled on the glories of Chítor. The city had recovered the sack, and new defenders had sprung up to replace those who had sacrificed themselves for her preservation. All that was wanting to augment her resources against the storms that were collecting on the Caucasus and the banks of the Oxus, was effected by Khúmbho, who, with Hamír's energy, Lakha's taste for the arts, and a genius comprehensive as either and more fortunate, succeeded in all his undertakings, and once more raised the "crimson banner" of Mewár upon the banks of the Caggar. Of the eighty-four fortresses for the defence of the state, thirty-two were erected by Khúmbho; and the famous Komulmír, or fortress of Khúmbho, is an imperishable example of his stupendous labours. This stronghold occupies the top of a lofty and precipitous hill, rising to a height of more than 3,000 feet above the sea. A massive wali, with numerous towers and pierced battlements encloses a space some miles in extent below. The ascent is very narrow, and four gateways have to be passed before the entrance to the fortress can be reached. The battlements rise, tier upon tier, to the summit of the hill, which is crowned with the Bádal Mahal, or "cloud-capped palace" of the Ránas. He also built a citadel on the peak of Abu, where he often resided. Its magazine and alarm-tower still bear his name;

Photo. by] [*Donald Macbeth, London*

THE FORTRESS OF KOMULMÍR

and in a rude temple the bronze effigies of Khúmbho and his father receive divine honours.

Besides these monuments of his genius, two consecrated to religion still survive; that of "Khúmbho Shaím" on Mount Abu, which, though worthy to attract notice elsewhere, is here eclipsed by a crowd of more interesting objects; and the other a temple erected in the Sádri pass, and one of the largest buildings existing. It is said to have cost upwards of a million pounds to build. It consists of three stories, and is supported by granite columns 40 feet in height. The interior is inlaid with mosaics of cornelian and agate. Khúmbho also attained some fame as an author, his principal work being a commentary on the *Gíta Govinda*, or "Divine Melodies." His wife, Míra Bai, a Rahtor princess, famed for her beauty and piety, was a writer of poetry, and many of her odes and hymns to the deity are yet preserved and admired.

Khúmbho's military achievements were many; but the most famous of them was his defeat of the combined armies of Málwa and Gujarát. It was towards the close of the Khilji dynasty that the satraps of Delhi began to shake off the imperial yoke, and to establish themselves as independent rulers. Five distinct kingdoms were created: Bíjapúr and Golconda in the Dekhan, and Jaunpúr, Málwa, and Gujarát in Hindustan proper. The two latter had attained considerable power when Khúmbho ascended the throne, and in the year 1440 they formed a league against him and invaded his kingdom. The Rána met them on the plains of Málwa bordering on his own state, at the head of 100,000 horse and foot and 14,000 elephants. The invaders were entirely defeated, and Mahmúd, the Khilji sovereign of Málwa, was carried captive to Chítor. Abul Fázil, the famous chronicler, relates this victory, and dilates on Khúmbho's greatness of soul in setting his enemy at liberty without ransom or gifts. The annals of Mewár, however, state that Mahmúd was confined six months in Chítor; and, that the trophies of conquest were retained, we have evidence from Bábar, who mentions recovering from the son of Rána Sanga the crown of the Málwa king. A column, the building of which occupied ten years, commemorates this victory, and the prowess of Khúmbho who saved his country when "shaking the earth, the lords of Gújur-khand and Málwa, with armies overwhelming as the ocean, invaded Medpat."

Khúmbho occupied the throne for half a century, and his reign was the most glorious in the history of Mewár. But the year which should have been a jubilee was marked by the foulest crime recorded in the annals. His life, which nature must soon have closed, was terminated by the poniard of an assassin—that assassin, his son!

v.—Ràna Sanga

UDA was the name of the parricide whose unnatural ambition bereft of life the author of his existence. But such is the detestation which marks this unusual crime that his name is left a blank in the annals, nor is he ever referred to except by the epithet *hatiáro*, "the murderer." Shunned by his kin, he was compelled to look abroad for succour to maintain himself on the throne polluted by his crime. He made the Deora prince independent in Abu, and bestowed Ajmír, Sámbur, and adjacent districts on the prince of Jodhpúr, as the price of their friendship. But though he bribed them with provinces, he felt that he could neither claim regard from, nor place any dependence upon them. He humbled himself before the king of Delhi, offering him a daughter in marriage to obtain his sanction to his authority; "but heaven manifested its vengeance to prevent this additional iniquity." He had scarcely quitted the audience chamber on taking leave of the king, when a flash of lightning struck him to the earth, whence he never rose.

The *hatiáro* was not only a parricide but a usurper, for the real heir-apparent was Raemal, who had been exiled by Khúmbho for an act of disrespect of which he had, unwittingly, been guilty. Having already defeated the forces of the pretender in a pitched battle, he had now little difficulty in establishing himself on the throne. He sustained the warlike reputation of his predecessors, and carried on interminable strife with Gheas-ud-dín of Málwa, defeating him in several encounters, after the last of which the Khilji king sued for peace. Raemal had three sons who, unhappily for their country and their father's repose, discarded fraternal affection for deadly hate. Each aimed at the throne, as did also their uncle Surájmal, and the feuds and dissensions consequent upon their rivalry kept the state in perpetual turmoil. The narration of these feuds, though it might afford a characteristic picture of the mode of life of the Rájpúts when their arms were not required against their country's foes, would prove both long and wearisome. In the end, all the rivals were slain except Sanga, the rightful heir-apparent, who lived to succeed his father in 1509.

So great had the prosperity of Mewár now become that Rána Sanga is described in the annals as the *kullus* (crown) on the pinnacle of her glory. From him we shall witness this glory on the wane; and though many rays of splendour illuminate her declining career, they serve but to gild the ruin. The imperial throne, held successively by the dynasties of Ghazni, Ghor, Khilji, and Lodi, was now shivered to pieces, and numerous petty thrones were constructed of its fragments. Mewár little dreaded these imperial puppets, "when Amurath to Amurath succeeded," and when four kings reigned simultaneously between Delhi and Benáres. The kings of Málwa, though leagued with those of Gujarát, could make no impression on Mewár when Sanga led her heroes. Eighty thousand horse, seven Rájas of the highest rank, nine Raos, and one hundred and four chieftains bearing the titles of

Ráwul and Ráwut, with five hundred war elephants, followed him to the field. The princes of Márwár and Ambar did him homage, and the Raos of Gwalior, Ajmír, Síkri, Raisen, Chanuéri, Bundi, Rampúra, and Abu, served him as tributaries, or held of him in fief.

In a short time, Sanga entirely allayed the disorders occasioned by the internal feuds of his family. He reorganised his forces, with which he always kept the field; and, ere called to contend with the descendants of Timúr, he had gained eighteen pitched battles against the kings of Delhi and Málwa. The Pílakhal river became the northern boundary of his territories, which extended to the Sindh river in the east, and to Málwa in the south, while his native hills formed an impregnable barrier in the west. Thus he swayed, directly or by control, the greater part of Rájasthán; and had not fresh hordes of Tartars and Usbecs from the prolific shores of the Oxus and Jaxartes again poured down on the devoted plains of Hindustan, the crown of the *Chacravarta* might once more have circled the brow of a Hindu, and the banner of supremacy, transferred from Indraprastha, might have waved from the battlements of Chítor. But Bábar arrived to rally the dejected followers of the Korán, and to collect them around his own victorious standard.

The Rájpút prince had a worthy antagonist in the king of Ferghána. Like Sanga, he had been trained in the school of adversity. In 1494, at the tender age of twelve, he succeeded to a kingdom; ere he was sixteen, he defeated several confederacies and conquered Samarkand, and in two short years, again lost and regained it. His life was a tissue of successes and reverses; at one moment hailed lord of the chief kingdoms of Transoxiana; at another, flying unattended, or putting all to hazard in desperate single combats. Driven from Ferghána, in despair he crossed the Hindu Kush, and in 1509 the Indus. Between the Punjab and Cábul he lingered seven years, ere he advanced to measure swords with Ibráhím of Delhi. Fortune returned to his standard; Ibráhím was slain, his army routed and dispersed, and Delhi and Agra opened their gates to the fugitive king. A year later, he ventured against the most powerful of his new antagonists, the Rána of Chitor.

It was in February 1527 that Bábar advanced from Agra and Sikri to oppose Sanga who, at the head of almost all the princes of Rájasthán, was marching to attack him. On the 11th of the month, according to the chronicles, Sanga encountered the advance guard of the Tartars, amounting to 1,500 men at Biána, and entirely destroyed them. Reinforcements met the same fate, and the news of the disaster, carried to the main body by the few who escaped with their lives, created the utmost dismay. Accustomed to reverses, Bábar adopted every precaution that a mind fertile in expedients could suggest to reassure the drooping spirits of his troops. He threw up entrenchments in which he placed his artillery, connecting his guns by chains, and, in the more exposed parts, *chevaux de frise*, united by leather ropes—a precaution continued in every subsequent change of position. Bábar was blockaded in his encampment for nearly a fortnight. Everything seemed to aid the Hindu cause. Even the Tartar astrologer asserted that, as Mars was in the west, whoever should engage coming from the opposite quarter was doomed to defeat. At length, unable to endure the state of almost total inactivity in which he was placed, Bábar determined to court the favour of heaven by renouncing his besetting sin, and thus, having merited superior aid, to extricate himself from his peril. The *naïveté* of his vow must be given in his own words. "On Monday," he says, "the 23rd of the first Jamádi, I had mounted to survey my posts, and in the course of my ride was seriously struck with the reflexion that I had always resolved, one time or another, to make an effectual repentance, and that some traces of a hankering after the renunciation of forbidden works had ever remained in my heart. I said to myself, 'O my soul, how long wilt thou continue to take pleasure in sin? Repentance is not unpalatable—taste it.' Thereupon, withdrawing myself from such temptation, I vowed never more to drink wine. Having sent for the gold and silver goblets, with all the other utensils used for drinking parties, I directed them to be broken, and renounced the use of wine, purifying my soul. The fragments of the goblets and other utensils, I directed to be divided amongst dervishes and the poor."[1]

But the destruction of the wine flasks would appear only to have added to the existing consternation. The desperate situation in which this mighty conqueror was placed is best described by himself. "At this time," he writes, "a general consternation and alarm prevailed among great and small. There was not a single person who uttered a manly word, nor an individual who delivered a courageous opinion. The Vazirs, whose duty it was to give good counsel,

[1] *Memoirs of Bábar*, translated by W. Erskine.

and the Amirs, who enjoyed the wealth of kingdoms, neither spoke bravely, nor was their counsel or deportment such as became men of firmness. During the whole course of this expedition, Khalifeh conducted himself admirably, and was unremitting and indefatigable in his endeavours to put everything in the best order. At length, observing the universal discouragement of my troops, and their total want of spirit, I formed my plan. I called an assembly of all the Amirs and officers, and addressed them: 'Noblemen and soldiers! Every man that comes into the world is subject to dissolution. When we are passed away and gone, God only survives, unchangeable. Whoever comes to the feast of life must, before it is over, drink from the cup of death. He who arrives at the inn of mortality, must one day inevitably take his departure from that house of sorrow, the world. How much better it is to die with honour than to live with infamy!

"'The most high God has been propitious to us, and has now placed us in such a crisis, that, if we fall in the field we die the death of martyrs; if we survive, we rise victorious, the avengers of the cause of God. Let us, then, with one accord, swear on God's holy word, that none of us will even think of turning his face from this warfare, nor desert from the battle and slaughter that ensues till his soul is separated from his body.'"[1]

[1] After this harangue, Bábar pushed on a few of his troops to skirmish with a party of the enemy, by way of taking an omen. "They took," he tells us, "a number of Pagans and cut off their heads, which they brought away. Malek Kásim also cut off and brought in some heads. He behaved extremely well. This incident raised the spirits of our army excessively." (*Memoirs of Bábar.*)

This stirring appeal produced the greatest enthusiasm. "Master and servant," he tells us, "small and great, all with emulation, swore in the form that I had given them. My plan succeeded to admiration, and its effects were instantly visible, far and near, on friend and foe." Why the Rána gave Bábar two whole weeks in which to reanimate the courage of his troops will probably never be explained. The delay proved as unfortunate for him as it did advantageous to the Tartar. It gave the latter the opportunity of proposing terms of peace, and this necessitated the presence in his camp of a Rájpút prince to conduct the negotiations. The chief of Raisen, by name Sillaidi, was chosen as the medium of communication. It was found impossible to arrange terms, and Sillaidi came back without a treaty, but with treachery in his heart.

Bábar was not a man to let the iron grow cold. Having stirred his troops to the necessary pitch of enthusiasm, he at once broke up his camp, and marched in order of battle to a position two miles in advance, the Rájpúts skirmishing up to his guns. The attack commenced by a furious onset on his centre and right wing, and for several hours the conflict was tremendous. The Tartar artillery made dreadful havoc in the close ranks of the Rájpút cavalry, who never fought with more devotion than on that fatal day. So ably were Bábar's guns served that his assailants could neither force his slight entrenchments nor reach the infantry which defended them. While the battle was still doubtful, the traitor of Raisen, who led the van, went over to Bábar, and Sanga, himself severely wounded and the choicest of his chieftains slain, was obliged to retreat from the field. Bábar had gained the day; but he had suffered so heavily that he was unable to follow up his victory. Triumphal pyramids were raised of the heads of the slain, and on a hillock overlooking the field of battle a tower of skulls was erected. The conqueror assumed the title of *Ghási*, which was retained for many generations by his descendants.

Sanga retreated towards the hills of Mewat, announcing his fixed determination never to enter Chítor but with victory. Had his life been spared to his country he might have redeemed the pledge; but the year of his defeat was the last of his existence, and he died at Buswa, on the frontier of Mewat, not without suspicion of poison. Rána Sanga was of the middle stature, but of great muscular strength, fair in complexion, with unusually large eyes, which appear to be peculiar to his descendants. He exhibited at his death but the fragments of a warrior. One eye was lost in a broil with his brother, an arm in an action with the Lodi king of Delhi, while he was a cripple owing to a limb having been broken by a cannon ball. From the sword or lance he counted eighty wounds on various parts of his body. He was celebrated for energetic enterprise, of which his successful storm of the almost impregnable Rinthambúr, though ably defended by the imperial general, Ali, is a celebrated instance. A cenotaph long marked the spot where the fire consumed his remains. He left seven sons, of whom the two elder died in nonage, and the third, Ratna, succeeded him.

Ratna possessed all the arrogance and martial valour of his race. He, too, determined to make the field his capital; and had he been spared to temper by experience the impetuosity of youth, would, doubtless have well seconded his father's resolution. But he was not destined to pass the age always dangerous to the turbulent and impatient Rájpút, ever courting strife if it would not find him. Before the death of his elder brother made him heir to Chítor, he had married by stealth, and by proxy, the daughter of Prithvi Ráj of Ambar, being represented at the nuptial ceremony by his double-edged sword. Unfortunately the affair was kept too secret; for the Hara prince of Búndi, in ignorance of what had taken place, demanded and obtained her to wife, and carried her to his capital. The bards of Búndi record this event with some pride, as evincing the power of their prince, who dared to solicit and obtain the hand of the bride of Chítor. The princes of Búndi had long been attached to the Sesodia house; and from the period when their common ancestors fought together on the banks of the Caggar against Shaháb-ud-dín they had silently grown to power under the wing of Mewár, and had often proved a strong plume in her pinion. When Ratna delayed to redeem his pledge, the maiden of Ambar saw no reason for disclosing her secret or of refusing the brave Hara, of whom fame spoke loudly. The unintentional offence sank deep into the heart of Ratna. He swore to be avenged; and in the accomplishment of his vow sacrificed his own life as well as that of his rival. The encounter which took place reflects little credit on the Sesodia prince; but it is worthy of narration as showing how in the Rájpút breast the desire for revenge could stifle every other feeling, even that of honour.

On the festival of the Ahairia the Rána invited himself to a hunt in the preserves of Búndi, and he took with him as his attendant the son of a Púrbía chieftain whose father had met his death at the hands of the Hara prince. The scene chosen for the sport was on the heights of Nandta, not far from the western bank of the Chambal, in whose glades every species of game, from the lordly lion to the timid hare, abounded. The troops were formed into line, and advanced through the jungle with the customary clamour, driving before them a promiscuous herd of the tenants of the forest. The princes had convenient stations assigned to them where they could spear the game as it passed. When the excitement was at its height the Rána whispered to his companion, "Now is the moment to slay the boar," and instantly an arrow sped from the bow of the Púrbía at the lord of Búndi. With an eagle's eye the Rao saw it coming, and turned it aside with his bow. This might very well have been an accident, but a second arrow from the same source convinced him there was treachery. Almost at the same moment the Rána darted at him on horseback, and cut him down with his *khanda*. The Rao fell, but, recovering, took his shawl and tightly bound up the wound, and as his foe was making off he cried aloud, "Escape you may, but you have sunk Mewár." The Púrbía, who followed his prince, when he saw the Hara bind up his wound, said, "The work is but half done"; and, like a coward, Ratna once more charged his wounded foe. As his arm was raised to finish the deed of shame, the Hara, with the strength of a wounded tiger, made a dying effort, and, catching his assailant by the robe, dragged him from his horse. Together they came to the ground, the Ráńa underneath. The Rao knelt upon his victim's chest, searching for his dagger with one hand, while with the other he held his victim by the throat. What a moment for revenge! He had strength enough left to raise his weapon and plunge it into the Rána's heart, and then, his vengeance satisfied, he sank lifeless on the body of his foe.

The Ahairia, to which allusion has just been made, and which proved fatal to more than one Rána of Mewár, merits some description. The word *ahairia* signifies a hunter, and is used to designate the festival of the spring hunt, which takes place in the month of Phálgan. The preceding day the Rána distributes to his chiefs and retainers dresses of a green colour, in which all appear habited on the morrow; and at the hour fixed by the astrologer they sally forth to slay a boar to Gouri, the Ceres of the Rájpúts. As success on this occasion portends future good fortune, no means are neglected to secure it, either by scouts previously discovering the lair, or by the desperate efforts of the hunters to slay the boar when roused. The prince and his sons, mounted on their best steeds, join in the chase, each animated by the desire to surpass his comrades in dexterity and courage. When the boar is started each cavalier urges forward his steed, and with lance or sword, regardless of rock, ravine, or tree, presses on the bristly quarry, whose knowledge of the country is of no avail when thus circumvented; and the ground soon reeks with gore, in which not unfrequently is mixed that of horse and rider.

The royal kitchen moves out on this occasion,

and in some chosen spot the repast is prepared, of which all partake, for the flesh of the hog is highly relished by the Rájpút. Having feasted and thrice slain their victim, they return in merry mood to the capital, whither the fame of their exploits has already preceded them.

vi.—Second Sack of Chítor and Accession of Udai Singh

THOUGH Ratna occupied the throne for only five years, he had the satisfaction of seeing the ex-king of Ferghána, the founder of the Mogul dynasty of India, leave the scene before him, and without the diminution of an acre of land to Mewár since the fatal day of Biána. He was succeeded by his brother, Bikramajít. This prince had all the turbulence of his race, without the redeeming qualities which had endeared his brother to his subjects. He was insolent, passionate, vindictive, and utterly regardless of the respect due to his proud nobles. Instead of appearing at their head, he passed his time amongst wrestlers and prize-fighters, on whom, and a multitude of *paiks*, or foot - soldiers, he lavished those gifts and favours to which the aristocratic Rájpúts, the equestrian order of Rájasthán, arrogated exclusive right. In this innovation he probably imitated his foes, who had learnt the value of infantry. The use of artillery was now becoming general, and the Moslems had perceived the necessity of foot for its protection. But, except in sieges, the Rájpút despised the new arm, preferring to fall with dignity from his steed, rather than to descend to an equality with his mercenary antagonist.

An open rupture was the consequence of such an innovation, and, to use the figurative expression for misrule, *Poppa Bai ká ráj*[1] was triumphant. The police were despised; the cattle carried off by free-booters from under the walls of Chítor; and when his cavaliers were ordered in pursuit, the Rána was tauntingly told to send his *paiks*.

Bahádur, Sultan of Gujarát, determined to take advantage of the Rájpút divisions, and to revenge the disgrace of his predecessor's defeat. Reinforced by the troops of Mandu, he marched against the Rána, then encamped in the Búndi territory. Though the force was overwhelming, yet, with the high courage belonging to his house, Bikramajít did not hesitate to give battle; but his mercenary bands were unable to withstand the Tartar onset, while his vassals and kin marched off in a body to defend Chítor and the posthumous son of Sanga Rána, still an infant.

There is a sanctity in the very name of Chítor, which from the earliest times never failed to secure her defenders. And now, when threatened again by the "barbarian," the bitterest feuds were forgotten, and every chieftain who could claim kinship with the house of Mewár came to pour out his blood in defence of the abode of his fathers. "The son of Búndi" came with a brave band of 500 Haras; the heir of Surájmal (son of the parricide Uda, who had made a kingdom for himself at Deola) brought a strong force of auxiliaries, as did also the chiefs of Sonigura and Deora, the Raos of Jhálawár and Abu, and many others from all parts of Rájasthán.

This was the most powerful effort hitherto made

1. The Government of Poppa Bai of ancient times, whose mismanaged sovereignty has given a proverb to the Rájpút.

against the state of Mewár by the sultans of Central India. European artillerists are recorded in the annals as brought to the subjugation of Chítor. The engineer is styled Labri Khán of Frengan, and to his skill Bahádur was indebted for the successful storm which ensued. He sprung a mine at the Bíka Rock, which blew up forty-five cubits of the ramparts, together with the bastion where the brave Haras were posted. The breach was bravely defended, and many assaults were repelled. To set an example of courageous devotion, the queen-mother, Jawáhi Bai, clad in armour, headed a sally, in which she was slain. Still the besiegers gained ground, and the last council convened was to concert means to save the infant son of Sanga from his imminent peril. But Chítor could only be defended by royalty, and again recourse was had to the expedient of crowning a king, as a sacrifice to the dignity of the presiding deity. The prince of Deola courted the insignia of destruction: the banner of Mewár floated over him, and the golden sun on its sable field never shone more refulgent than when the *changi*[1] was raised, amid the shouts of the defenders, over the head of the son of Surájmal. The infant Udai Singh was

[1] At Udaipúr the sun has universal precedence; his portal (*Surya-pol*) is the chief entrance to the city; his name gives dignity to the chief apartment or hall (*Surya-mahal*) of the palace; and from the balcony of the sun (*Surya-gokra*) the descendant of Ráma shows himself in the dark monsoon as the sun's representative. A huge painted sun of gypsum, in high relief, with gilded rays, adorns the hall of audience, and in front of it is the throne. As already mentioned, the sacred standard bears his image, as does that Scythic part of the regalia called the *changi*, a disc of black felt or ostrich feathers, with a plate of gold to represent the sun in its centre, borne upon a pole. The royal parasol is termed *kirnia*, in allusion to its shape, like a ray (*kiran*) of the orb. For a representation of the *changi*, see frontispiece.

placed in safety with the prince of Búndi, and, while materials for the *johur* were preparing, the garrison put on their saffron robes. There was little time for the pyre. The bravest had fallen in defending the breach, now completely exposed. Combustibles were quickly heaped in reservoirs and magazines excavated in the rock, under which gunpowder was strewed. Kurnavati, mother of the prince, led the procession of willing victims to their doom, and 13,000 females were thus swept, in a moment, from the record of life. The gates were thrown open, and the Deola chief, at the head of the survivors, with a blind and impotent despair, rushed on his fate. Bahádur must have been appalled at the horrid spectacle which the interior of the fortress presented. To use the emphatic words of the annalist, "the last day of Chítor had arrived." Every clan lost its chief, and the choicest of its warriors. During the siege and in the storm 32,000 Rájpúts were slain. This was the second *saca* of Chítor.

Bahádur had remained but a fortnight in Chítor when the advance of Humáyun, who had received the gift of the bracelet from Queen Kurnavati, and was therefore pledged to champion her cause, warned him to retire. The custom here alluded to played, on more than one occasion, an important part in the history of Rájasthán, and merits more than a passing reference. The festival of the *rakhi* (bracelet) takes place in the spring, and, whatever its origin, it is one of the few when an intercourse of gallantry of the most delicate nature is established between the fair sex and the cavaliers of Rájasthán. At this season the Rájpút dame sends a bracelet, either by her handmaid or the family priest, to the knight of her choice. With the *rakhi* she confers the title of adopted brother; and, while its acceptance secures to her all the protection of a *cavalier servant*, scandal itself never suggests any other tie to his devotion. He may hazard his life in her cause, and yet never receive a smile in reward, for he cannot even see the fair object who has constituted him her defender. But there is a charm in the mystery of such connection, and no honour is more highly esteemed than that of being the *rakhi-band bhai*, or "bracelet-bound brother," of a princess. The intrinsic value of the pledge is never looked to, nor is it necessary that the gift should be costly, though it varies with the means and rank of the donor, and may be of flock silk and spangles, or of gold chains and gems. The acceptance of the pledge and its return is by the *katchli*, or corset, of simple silk or satin, or of gold brocade and pearls. A whole province has often accompanied the *katchli*.

The courteous delicacy of this custom appealed to the chivalrous nature of Humáyun, and he was so pleased at receiving the bracelet from the princess Kurnavati, which invested him with the title of her brother, and protector to her infant Udai Singh, that he pledged himself to her service, "even if the demand were the castle of Rinthambúr." It was not until her Amazonian sister, the Rahtor queen, was slain, that Kurnavati demanded the fulfilment of the pledge. Humáyun proved himself a true knight, and even abandoned his conquests in Bengal to succour Chítor. He expelled the troops of Bahádur from the city, took Mandu by assault, and, as a punishment for the part her chief had played in allying himself with the king of Gujarát, he sent for the Rána Bikramajít whom, following their own notions of investiture, he girt with a sword in the captured citadel of his foe.

Bikramajít, though restored to his capital, had gained nothing by adversity; or, to employ the words of the annalist, "experience had brought no wisdom." He renewed all his former insolence to his nobles, and so entirely threw aside his own dignity as to strike in open court Karamchand of Ajmír, the protector of his father, Sanga, in his misfortunes. The assembly rose with one accord at this indignity to their order and repaired straightway to Banbír, the natural son of Sanga's brother Prithvi Ráj, and offered to seat him on the throne of Chítor. Banbír had the virtue, or the cunning, to resist the solicitation, and it was only when the nobles painted the dangers which threatened their country if their chief at such a period had not their confidence, that he gave his consent.

A few hours of sovereignty, however, sufficed to check those "compunctuous visitings" which assailed Banbír ere he assumed its trappings, with which he found himself so little encumbered that he was content to wear them for life. Whether this was the intention of the nobles who set aside the unworthy son of Sanga, there is abundant reason to doubt; and as Banbír is subsequently branded with the epithet of "usurper," it was probably limited to investing him with the executive authority during the minority of Udai Singh. Banbír, however, only awaited the approach of night to remove with his own hands the obstacle to his ambition. Udai Singh was not yet six years of age. He had gone to sleep after his rice and milk, when his nurse was alarmed by screams from the *ráwula*, or seraglio, and the *bári* (barber), coming in to remove the remains of the dinner, informed her of the cause, the assassination of the Rána.

Aware that one murder was the precursor of another, the faithful nurse put her charge into a fruit basket, and, covering it with leaves, delivered it to the *bári*, enjoining him to escape with it from the fort. Scarcely had she had time to substitute her own son in the room of the prince, when Banbír, entering, enquired for him. Her lips refused their office. She pointed to the bed, and beheld the murderous steel buried in the heart of her child. The little victim to fidelity was burnt amidst the tears of the household, who supposed that their grief was given to the last pledge of the illustrious Sanga. The nurse, a Rájpútni of the Khíchí tribe, having consecrated with her tears the ashes of her child, hastened after that she had preserved. But well had it been for Mewár had the poniard fulfilled its intention, and had the annals never recorded the name of Udai Singh in the catalogue of her princes.

The faithful barber was awaiting the nurse in the bed of the Beris river, some miles west of Chítor, and fortunately the child had remained asleep until he had descended from the city. They set out for Deola, and sought refuge with Singh Rao, the successor of Bagh-ji, who fell for Chítor. But the prince, dreading the consequences of detection, refused the fugitives an asylum. They proceeded to Dongarpúr which, like Deola, was ruled by a prince closely allied to the house of Chítor. Here, too, they met with disappointment, the prince pleading the danger which threatened himself and the child in so feeble a sanctuary. Pursuing a circuitous route through the intricate valleys of the Arávalli, and aided by the protection of the wild but hospitable Bhíls, they gained Komulmír. The resolution which the nurse had formed was as bold as it was judicious. She demanded an interview with the Governor, Assa Sah, and, this being granted, she placed the child in his lap, and bade him "guard the life of his sovereign." Assa Sah was perplexed and alarmed; but his mother, who was present, upbraided him for his scruples. "Fidelity," she said, "never looks at dangers and difficulties. He is your master, the son of Sanga, and by God's blessing the result will be glorious." So Udai Singh found a refuge at Komulmír, where he was given out to be the nephew of Assa.

The fact of Udai Singh's existence remained hidden for seven years; and the secret was eventually betrayed by his aristocratic appearance and bearing. On the occasion of the visit of the Sonigurra chief, Udai Singh was sent to receive him, and the dignified manner in which he performed the duty convinced the chief that "he was no nephew to the Sah." Rumour spread the tale, and brought not only the nobles of Mewár, but many adjacent chiefs, to hail the son of Rána Sanga. All doubt was finally removed by the testimony of the nurse, and her coadjutor the barber. A court was formed, and the faithful Assa resigned his trust, and placed the prince in the lap of the Kotário Chohan, as the "great ancient" among the nobles of Mewár, who had throughout been acquainted with the secret, and who, to dissipate any doubts that might yet remain, "ate off the same plate with him." Udai received the *tíka* of Chítor in the castle of Khúmbho, and the homage of nearly all the chiefs of Mewár.

Meanwhile, things had been progressing but indifferently well with Banbír. He had not borne himself meekly since his advancement. Having seized on the dignity of the legitimate monarchs of Chítor, he wished to ape all their customs; and even had the effrontery to punish as an insult the refusal of one of the proud sons of Chonda to take the *dúnah* from his bastard hand. The *dúnah* is a portion of the dish of which the prince partakes, sent by his own hand to whomsoever he honours at the banquet. At the *rassora*, or refectory, the chiefs who are admitted to dine in the presence of their sovereign are seated according to their rank. The repast is one of those occasions when an easy familiarity is permitted, which though unrestrained, never exceeds the bounds of etiquette, and the habitual reverence due to their father and prince. When he sends, by the steward of the kitchen, a portion of the dish before him, or a little from his own *khansa*, or plate, all eyes are guided to the favoured mortal, whose good fortune is the subject of subsequent conversation. To such an extent is the privilege yet carried, and such importance is attached to the personal character of the princes of Mewár, that the test of regal legitimacy in Rájasthán is admission to eat from the same plate with the Rána; and to the refusal of this honour to the great Mán Singh of Ambar, may be indirectly ascribed the ruin of the state.

It may, therefore, be conceived with what contempt

the haughty nobility of Chítor received the mockery of honour from the hand of this "fifth son of Mewár"; and the Chondáwat chief had the boldness to add to his refusal that "an honour from the hand of a true son of Bappa Ráwul becomes a disgrace when proffered by the offspring of the handmaid, Sítulsíni." The defection soon became general, and all repaired to the valley of Komulmír to hail the legitimate son of Mewár. A caravan of 500 horses and 10,000 oxen, laden with merchandise from Kutch, the dower of Banbír's daughter, guarded by 1,000 horsemen, was plundered in the passes; a signal intimation of the decay of the chief's authority, and affording a welcome supply for the celebration of the nuptials of Udai Singh with the daughter of the Rao of Jhálawár. Deserted by all, Banbír held out in the capital; but his minister admitted, under the garb of a reinforcement with supplies, a thousand resolute adherents of the prince. The keepers of the gates were surprised and slain, and the reign of Udai Singh was proclaimed. Banbír was permitted to retire with his family and his wealth. He sought refuge in the Dekhan, and the Bhonsla's of Nágpúr are said to derive their origin from this spurious branch of Chítor.

vii.—Third and Last Sack of Chítor

RÁNA UDAI SINGH ascended the throne in 1541, amidst great rejoicings. The song of triumph, which was composed for the occasion, is yet a favourite at Udaipúr, and on the festival of Gouri, the Ceres of Rájasthán, the females still chant the "farewell to Komulmír." But the ruin of Mewár, which set in with Sanga's death, and was accelerated by the fiery valour of Ratna and the capricious conduct of Bikramajít, was completed by an anomaly in her annals: a coward succeeding a bastard to guide the destinies of the Sesodias. Udai Singh had not one quality of a sovereign, and, wanting martial virtue—the common heritage of his race—he was destitute of all. Yet he might have slumbered life away in inglorious repose during the lifetime of Humáyun, or the contentions of the Pathán usurpers who came after. But, unfortunately for Rájasthán, a prince was then rearing who forged fetters for the Hindu race which enthralled it for ages. Time has broken them asunder, but their indelible marks remain, not like the galley-slave's, physical and exterior, but deep mental scars never to be effaced.

In the same year that the song of joy was raised in the cloud-capped palace of Komulmír, for the deliverance of Udai Singh, there was born, in an oasis of the Indian desert, an infant destined to be the most powerful monarch that ever swayed sceptre of Hindustan. Akbar the Great first saw the light amid scenes of hardship and affliction; his father a fugitive, the diadem torn from his brows, and its recovery more improbable than had been its acquisition by Bábar. Humáyun trained his son, as his own father had trained him, in the school of adversity; and the greatest of the great Moguls passed the first twelve years of his life surrounded by every trial of fortune.

During this short period, the imperial throne at Delhi, which the Pathán Lion had wrested from his grasp, was occupied in succession by no less than six kings, of whom the last, Sikandar, became involved in civil broils which rapidly undermined his power. Humáyun no sooner saw the tide of events set counter to his foe, than he crossed the Indus and advanced upon Sirhind, where the Pathán soon met him with a tumultuous array. The impetuosity of young Akbar brought on a general engagement, which the veterans deemed madness. Not so Humáyun. He gave over the command to his boy, who, by his heroism, so excited all ranks that they despised the numbers of the enemy and gained a glorious victory. This was the presage of Akbar's future fame; for he was then but twelve years of age, the same period of life at which his grandfather Bábar maintained himself on the throne of Ferghána. Six years later, this same youth was the uncontrolled ruler of the Mogul empire.

Scarcely was Akbar seated on the throne, when Delhi and Agra were wrested from him, and a nook of the Punjab constituted all his empire. But by the energetic valour of the great Bairam Khán, his lost sovereignty was regained with equal rapidity, and established by the wisdom of this Sulla of

Hindustan on a rock. Cálpi, Chandéri, Callingar, all Bandalkand and Málwa were soon attached to the empire; and then the conqueror turned his attention towards the Rájpúts. He advanced against the Rahtors, and stormed and took Mairtia, the second city in Márwár. Rája Bharmal of Ambar anticipated matters by enrolling himself and his son, Bhagwán Dás, among Akbar's vassals, gave him a daughter to wife, and held his country as a fief of the empire. The rebellions of the Usbec nobles checked for a time his designs on Rájasthán; but these were soon quelled, and the imperial army was free to advance to the subjugation of the prince of Chítor.

Akbar was the real founder of the empire of the Moguls, the first successful conqueror of Rájpút independence. Though he led their princes captive, his virtues were such that he was able to gild the fetters with which he bound them. But generations of the martial races were cut off by his sword, and lustres rolled away ere his conquests were sufficiently confirmed to permit him to exercise the benevolence of his nature, and obtain by the universal acclaim of the conquered the proud title of *Jaggat Gur*, the "guardian of mankind." He was long ranked with Shaháb-ud-dín, Allah, and other instruments of destruction, and with every just claim. Like these, he constructed from the altars of Eklinga a pulpit for the Korán. Yet he finally succeeded in healing the wounds his ambition had inflicted, and received from millions that mead of praise which no other of his race ever obtained.

The absence of the kingly virtues in the sovereign of Mewár filled to the brim the bitter cup of her destiny. The guardian goddess of the Sesodias had promised never to abandon the rock of her pride while a descendant of Bappa Ráwul devoted himself to her service. In the first assault by Allah, twelve crowned heads had defended the "crimson banner." In the second, the crown of martyrdom was worn by the brave chieftain of Deola. But in this, the third and greatest struggle, no regal victim was forthcoming, and the mysterious tie which united the Gehlote to the throne of Chítor was severed for ever. The enchanted fortress, "the abode of regality, which for a thousand years reared her head above all the cities of Hindustan," was henceforward regarded as indefensible, and became a refuge to the wild beasts which sought cover in her temples.

Ferishta mentions but one enterprise against Chítor—that of its capture; but the annals record another when Akbar was compelled to relinquish his undertaking. The successful defence is attributed to the masculine courage of the Rána's concubine queen, who headed the sallies into the heart of the Mogul camp, and on one occasion to the emperor's headquarters. The imbecile Rána proclaimed that he owed his deliverance to her, when the chiefs, indignant at this imputation on their courage, conspired and put her to death. Internal discord invited Akbar to re-invest Chítor; he had just attained his twenty-fifth year, and was desirous of the renown of capturing it. The site of the royal *úrdú*, or camp, is still pointed out. It extended from the village of Pandaoli along the high road to Bussi, a distance of ten miles. The headquarters of Akbar are marked by a pyramidal column of marble, to which tradition

Photo by] [*Donald Macbeth, London*

AN INTERIOR VIEW OF CHİTOR.

[*p.* 68

has assigned the name, *Akbar ká díwa*, or Akbar's lamp.[1]

Scarcely had Akbar sat down before Chítor, when the Rána was compelled (say the annals) to quit it; but the necessity and his wishes were in unison. It lacked not, however, brave defenders. Sahidás, at the head of a numerous band of the descendants of Chonda, was at his post, "the gate of the sun"; there he fell resisting the entrance of the foe, and there his altar stands on the brow of the rock, which was moistened by his blood. Ráwut Deola led the "sons of Sanga." The feudatory chiefs of Baidla and Kotário, descendants of Prithvi Ráj of Delhi, the Tuár prince of Gwalior, the Rao of Jhálawár, the chief of Deola, and many others inspired their contingents with their brave example, and sacrificed their lives for the sacred city. Though deprived of the stimulous that would have been given had their prince been a witness of their deeds, heroic achievements, such as those before recorded, were conspicuous on this occasion; and many a fair form threw the buckler over the scarf, and led the most desperate sorties.

But the names which shine brightest in this gloomy page of the annals of Mewár, names immortalised by Akbar's own pen, are those of Jaimal of Bednor and Patta of Kailwa, both of the sixteen superior vassals of Chítor. The first was a Rahtor of the Mairtia house, the bravest of the brave clans of

[1] The pillar is still as perfect as when constructed, being of immense blocks of white limestone, closely fitted to each other. Its height is 30 feet, its base a square of 12 feet, and its summit of 4. On it was placed a huge concave vessel filled with fire, which served as a night beacon to the ambulatory city, and as a guide to the foragers.

Márwár; the other was head of the Jugáwats, another grand shoot from Chonda. Their names, "Jaimal and Patta," always inseparable, are as household words in Mewár, and will be honoured while the Rájpút retains a shred of his inheritance or a spark of his ancient recollections. When Sahidás fell at "the gate of the sun," the command devolved on Patta of Kailwa. He was only sixteen. His father had fallen in the last siege, and his mother had survived but to rear this the sole heir of her house. Like the Spartan mother of old, she commanded him to put on the saffron robe, and to die for Chítor; but, surpassing the Grecian dame, she illustrated her precept by example; and, lest thoughts for one dearer than herself might dim the lustre of Kailwa, she armed his young bride with a lance, and the defenders of Chítor saw the fair princess descend the rock and fall fighting by the side of her brave mother.

When their wives and daughters performed such deeds, the Rájpúts became reckless of life. Patta was slain; and Jaimal, who had taken his place, was grievously wounded. Seeing there was no hope of salvation he resolved to signalise the end of his career. The fatal *johur* was commanded, while 8,000 Rájpúts ate the last *bira*[1] together, and put on their saffron robes. The gates were thrown open, the work of destruction commenced, and few survived to "stain the yellow mantle" by inglorious surrender. All the heads of clans, both home and foreign, fell, and 1,700 of the immediate kin of the prince sealed their

[1] The areca nut wrapped in the leaf of the *betel*, which is always presented to departing guests.

duty to their country with their lives. Nine queens, five princesses, with two infant sons, and the families of all the chieftains who took part in the defence perished in the flames, or at the hands of the enemy. Their divinity had, indeed, forsaken them! The rock of their strength was despoiled; their temples and palaces dilapidated; and, to complete the humiliation and his own triumph, Akbar bereft the city of all the symbols of sovereignty—the *nakaras*, or grand kettle-drums, whose reverberations proclaimed, for miles round, the entrance and exit of her princes; the candelabras from the shrine of the "Great Mother," who girt Bappa Ráwul with the sword with which he conquered Chítor; and, in mockery of her misery, he carried away her portals to adorn his projected capital, Akbarábád.

Akbar claimed the honour of the death of Jaimal by his own hand: the fact is recorded by Abul Fázil and by the Emperor Jahángír, who conferred on the matchlock, which aided his father to this distinction, the title of *Singrám*. But the conqueror of Chítor evinced a more exalted sense of the merits of his foes in erecting statues in honour of Jaimal and Patta at the most conspicuous entrance of his palace at Delhi. They still occupied this distinguished position when Bernier was in India; and, in a letter written from Delhi in 1663, that illustrious traveller remarks: "These two great elephants, together with the two resolute men sitting on them do at the first entry into the fortress make an impression of I know not what greatness and awful terror." When the Carthagenian gained the battle of Cannae, he measured his success by the bushels of rings taken from the fingers of the equestrian

Romans who fell on that memorable field. Akbar estimated his by the quantity of cordons of distinction taken from the necks of the Rájpúts, and seventy-four and a half *man*, or about five hundredweight, is the recorded amount. To eternise the memory of this disaster the number 74½ is *tilac*, that is, accursed. Marked on a banker's letter in Rájasthán it is the strongest of seals, for "the sin of the sack of Chítor" is invoked on him who violates a letter under the safeguard of this mysterious number.

When Udai Singh abandoned Chítor, he found refuge in the valley of the Girwoh in the Arávalli, close to the retreat of his great ancestor, Bappa, ere he conquered Chítor. At the entrance to this valley, several years previously, he had formed the lake still called after him, Udai Ságar, and he now raised a dyke between the hills which dammed up another stream. On the cluster of hills adjoining, he built the small palace called Nauchoki, around which edifices soon arose to which he gave his own name, Udaipúr, henceforth the capital of Mewár.

Four years had Udai Singh survived the loss of his capital when he expired at Gogúnda, at the early age of forty-two. His last act was to entail contention upon his sons, of whom he left twenty-five; for, setting aside the established law of primogeniture, he proclaimed his favourite son Jagmal his successor. In Mewár there is no interregnum. The ceremony of mourning is held at the house of the family priest, while the palace is decked out in honour of the new ruler. While his brothers and the nobles attended the funeral pyre, Jagmal took possession of the throne in the infant capital. But even as the trumpet sounded, and the heralds called aloud, "Let the king live for ever," a cabal was formed round the bier of his father. It will be borne in mind that Udai Singh had espoused the daughter of the Rao of Jhálawár, and that chief had little difficulty in inducing Kistna, the "great ancient of Mewár" and the leader of her nobles, to support the rightful cause of his grandson, Partáp. Jagmal was just about to enter the *rassora*, and Partáp was saddling for his departure, when Kistna appeared, accompanied by the ex-prince of Gwalior. Each chief took an arm of Jagmal, and, with gentle violence, guided him to a seat in the front of the "cushion" he had occupied, the old noble remarking, "You made a mistake, Maháráj; that place belongs to your brother." Partáp was then girt with the sword, and hailed by all present the king of Mewár. No sooner was the ceremony concluded, than the young prince reminded them that it was the festival of the Ahairia, and that ancient customs should not be forgotten; "therefore, to horse, and slay a boar to Gouri, and take the omen for the coming year." They slew abundance of game, and, in the mimic field of war, the nobles who surrounded the gallant Partáp anticipated happier days for Mewár.

It may not be out of place if we here give some account of the shrine of Eklinga, the tutelary deity of Mewár, and his consort, the lion-born goddess, whose wrath was fraught with such signal disaster to their followers.

The shrine of Eklinga is situated in a defile about six miles north of Udaipúr. The hills around it on all sides are of the primitive formation, and their scarped summits, the abode of countless swarms of wild bees, are clustered with honey-combs. Abundant springs of water keep alive the various shrubs, the flowers of which are acceptable to the deity, especially the *kinar* or oleander, which grows in great luxuriance on the Arávalli. It would be difficult to convey a just idea of a temple so complicated in its details. It is of the type usually styled a pagoda, and, like all the ancient temples of Siva, its *sikra*, or pinnacle, is pyramidal. The various orders of Hindu sacred architecture are distinguished by the form of the *sikra*, which is the portion springing from and surmounting the perpendicular walls of the body of the building, and in those dedicated to Siva is invariably pyramidal, its sides conforming to the shape of the base, which is either square or oblong. The apex is crowned with an ornamental figure of an urn, a bull, or a lion, which is called the *kullus*. The fane of Eklinga is of white marble, and of ample dimensions. Beneath a vaulted roof, supported by columns, is the brazen bull, Nanda; it is cast, of the natural size, and of excellent proportions. The figure is perfect, except where the shot or hammer of an infidel invader has penetrated its hollow flank in search of treasure. The high priest of Eklinga, like all his order, is doomed to celibacy, and the office is continued by adopted disciples. The members of the order are styled Goswámi, which signifies one who has control over the senses. The distinguishing mark of the priests of Siva is a crescent on the forehead; the hair is braided and forms a tiara round the head, and with its folds a chaplet of the lotus seed is often entwined. They smear the body with ashes, and wear garments dyed an orange hue. They live in monasteries scattered over the country, possess lands, beg, and serve for pay when called upon. The shrine is endowed with twenty-four large villages from the fisc of Mewár, besides parcels of land from the estates of the chieftains. The Ránas, as *diwáns* of Siva, supersede the high priest in his duties whenever they visit the temple.

This privilege has belonged to the Ránas since the days of their famous ancestor Bappa, who acquired it in the following manner. While pasturing the sacred kine in the valley of Nagindra, the princely shepherd was suspected of appropriating the milk of a favourite cow to his own use. He was distrusted and watched, and, though indignant, he admitted that there were grounds for suspicion from the habitual dryness of the brown cow when she entered the pens at night. One day, being determined to solve the mystery, he tracked the animal to a narrow dell, where he beheld her spontaneously yield her store of milk for the benefit of an aged hermit, who proved to be none other than Haríta, the high priest of Eklinga. Bappa related to the sage all that he knew of himself, received his blessing, and retired; but he came every day to visit him, ministering to his needs, and gathering such wild flowers as were an acceptable offering to the deity. In return, he received lessons in morality, and was initiated into the mysterious rites of Siva. At length, he was invested with the triple thread by the hands of the sage, who became his spiritual adviser, and bestowed upon him the title "regent of Eklinga." Bappa had proofs that his attentions to the sage and his devotions to the deity were favourably regarded, for the lion-born goddess herself appeared before him. From her hand he received his celestial panoply—a lance, a bow, a quiver and arrows, a shield, and a sword, which last the goddess girded on him with her own hand, while he swore eternal fidelity and devotion. The temple of Eklinga was erected on the very spot where the goddess appeared to Bappa, and the present high priest traces sixty-six descents from Haríta to himself.

Before passing on to the reign of Partáp, the most renowned of all the Rána's of Mewár, we will glance for a few moments at the condition of Rájpútána during the period of Mogul supremacy, and the policy initiated by Akbar, and followed by the two monarchs who succeeded him, for the consolidation of the empire. The existence of a number of powerful and independent principalities, constantly at feud with one another, and ready at a moment's notice to combine against a common foe, was not only a constant menace to the security of the imperial throne, but a serious hindrance to the establishment of any settled form of government. The subjugation of Rájpútána was, therefore, one of the first undertakings to which the astute and energetic son of Humáyun turned his attention.

The Rájpút princes soon realised that the imperial power was irresistible, and, rather than suffer political annihilation, preferred, in most cases, to make the best terms they could with their not ungenerous foe. One by one they surrendered to Akbar their kingdoms, receiving them back with a *sanad*, or grant, thereby acknowledging him as lord paramount, and themselves as fiefs of the empire. On these occasions, they received the *khilát*[1] of honour and investiture, consisting of elephants, horses, arms, and jewels, and to their hereditary title of prince was added by the emperor that of *mansabdár*, or military commander. Besides this acknowledgment of supremacy, they offered *nazarána*[2] and paid homage, engaging to attend the royal presence when required, at the head of a stipulated number of their vassals. The emperor presented them with a standard, kettle-drums, and other insignia, which headed the contingent of each prince.

The splendour of such an array, whether in the field or at the palace, can scarcely be conceived. Though Humáyun had gained the services of several of the Rájpút princes, their aid had been uncertain. It was reserved for his wise and magnanimous son to induce them to become at once the ornament and the support of his throne. The power which he consolidated, and knew so well how to wield, was irresistible; while the beneficence of his disposition and the wisdom of his policy maintained in security whatever his might conquered. He knew that a constant exhibition of authority would be both ineffectual and dangerous, and that the surest way to gain a hold on the loyalty and esteem of the conquered was to give them a personal interest in the support of the monarchy.

[1] A *khilat* is a presentation made to a person invested with a new office, or in confirmation of one he already holds. The word signifies, in Arabic, a dress or robe of honour. But a *khilat* may consist of horses, jewels, money, or any articles of value, though in most cases a turban and a shawl form part of the gift.

[2] *Nazarána* are gifts offered by an inferior to a superior as a mark of respect. Such gifts may be accepted, or merely touched with the hand and returned.

But Akbar carried his scheme of conciliation yet further. He determined to unite the pure blood of the Rájpúts to the scarcely less noble stream which flowed from Chenghiz Khán through Timúr and Bábar to himself, calculating that they would more readily yield obedience to a prince who claimed kindred with them, than to one of undiluted Tartar blood. Ambar, the nearest state to Delhi, and the most exposed, was the first to unite itself to the empire by this means; and subsequently the practice became so common that some of the most celebrated of the Mogul emperors were the offspring of Rájpút princesses. The last Mogul sovereign to marry a Rájpút princess was Farrukhsiyar, who espoused the daughter of Rája Ajít Singh of Márwar.

Of the four hundred and sixteen *mansabdárs* of Akbar's empire forty-seven were Rájpúts, and the aggregate of their quotas amounted to fifty-three thousand horse. Of these, seventeen held *mansabs* of from two thousand to five thousand horse, and thirty from one hundred to two thousand. The princes of Ambar, Márwár, Bíkanír, Búndi, Jaisalmír, and Bandalkand held *mansabs* of above one thousand; but Ambar alone, being allied to the royal family, had the dignity of five thousand. Such duties, though in the first place compulsory, soon came to be coveted and regarded as honourable; and thus Akbar gained a double victory, securing the good opinion as well as the swords of the Rájpúts in his aid. A judicious perseverance would have rendered the throne of Timúr immovable; but the beneficence and toleration of Akbar, Jahángír, and Shah Jahán were lost sight of by the bigoted and blood-thirsty Aurangzeb, who, though able by his commanding

Photo by] *Donald Macbeth, London*

A RÁJPÚT SOLDIER

genius to hold his empire together during his lifetime, extinguished in his Hindu subjects every sentiment of loyalty and affection which the wisdom of his predecessors had kindled. This affection withdrawn, and the weakness of Farrukhsiyar substituted for the strength of Aurangzeb, the already tottering throne of the Moguls crumbled to pieces. Predatory warfare and spoliation rose on its ruins, and a general scramble for territory ensued. The Rájpút princes thought of nothing but re-establishing their independence and adding to their lands and power. Old jealousies were not lessened by the part which each had played in the hour of ephemeral greatness; and the prince of Mewár, who had preserved his blood uncontaminated, was at once an object of respect and envy to those who had forfeited the first pretensions of a Rájpút. The new lands acquired by these princes whilst basking in court favour had made them equal, if not superior, in power to the Rána, and they desired that the dignities they had received from the sons of Timúr should appear as distinguished as his ancient title. Hence, while one inscribed on his seal, "the exalted in dignity, a prince among princes," and another, "lord of the lords of Ind," the princes of Mewár preserved their royal simplicity, and the sole designation of the chief who, in 1817, allied himself to the British Government was "Mahárána Bhím Singh, son of Arsi."

viii.—Rána Partáp

Partáp succeeded to the titles and renown of an illustrious house, without a capital, without resources, his kindred and clans weakened and dispirited. Yet, possessed by the noble spirit of his race, he meditated the recovery of Chítor, the vindication of the honour of his house, and the restoration of its power. Elevated with this design, he hurried into conflict with his powerful antagonist, nor stopped to calculate the means which were opposed to him. Accustomed to read in his country's annals the splendid deeds of his forefathers, he trusted that fortune might co-operate with his efforts to overturn the unstable throne of Delhi. But while he gave rein to these lofty aspirations, his crafty opponent was undermining them by a scheme of policy which, when disclosed, filled his heart with anguish. The wily Mogul arrayed against Partáp his kindred in faith as well as in blood. The princes of Márwár, Ambar, Bíkanír, and even Búndi, late his ally, took part with Akbar. Nay, even his own brother, Ságarji, deserted him, and received, as the price of his treachery, the ancient capital of his race and the title which that possession conferred.

But the magnitude of the peril confirmed the fortitude of Partáp, who vowed, in the words of the bard, "to make his mother's milk resplendent." Single-handed, for a quarter of a century, he withstood the combined efforts of the empire: at one time carrying destruction into the plains, at another, flying from rock to rock, feeding his family from the fruits of his native hills, and rearing the nursling hero Amra amidst savage beasts and scarce less savage men, a fit heir to his prowess and revenge. The bare idea that the son of Bappa Ráwul should bow the head to mortal man was insupportable; and he spurned every overture which had submission for its basis, or the degradation of uniting his family by marriage with the Tartar. The brilliant acts he achieved during that period live in every valley. To recount them all, or relate the hardships he sustained, would be to pen what would be described as a romance by those who have not traversed the country where tradition is yet eloquent of his exploits, nor conferred with the descendants of his chiefs, who cherish the recollections of the deeds of their ancestors, and melt, as they recite them, into manly tears.

Partáp was nobly supported; and though wealth and fortune tempted the fidelity of his retainers, not one was found base enough to desert him. The sons of Jaimal shed their blood in his cause along with the descendants of Patta; the Chondáwats, the descendants of Chonda, redoubled their devotion to the fallen house; the chief of Dailwára pressed to his standard, as did many others, attracted by the very desperation of his fortunes. To commemorate the desolation of Chítor, Partáp interdicted to himself and his followers every article of luxury or pomp, until the insignia of her glory should be redeemed. The gold and silver vessels were laid aside for *pateras* of leaves, their beards were left untouched, and their beds were of straw; and to mark yet more distinctly their fallen state, the martial *nakaras*, which always sounded in the van of the battle or procession, were commanded to follow in the rear. This last sign of the depression of Mewár survives to this day. The beard of the prince is still untouched by the shears, and though he eats off gold and silver, and sleeps on a bed, he places leaves beneath the one and straw under the other.

With the aid of his chiefs Partáp remodelled his government, adapting it to the exigencies of the times and to his slender resources. New grants were issued with regulations defining the service required. Komulmír, now the seat of his government, was strengthened, as well as Gogúnda and other mountain fortresses. Being unable to keep the field in Mewár, he followed the system of his ancestors, and commanded his subjects, on pain of death, to retire to the mountains. Many tales are told of the unrelenting severity with which he enforced obedience to his stern policy. Frequently, with a few horse, he issued forth to see that his edicts were obeyed. The silence of the desert prevailed in the plains; grass usurped the place of the waving corn; the highways were choked with the thorny *babúl*[1]; and beasts of prey made their abode in the habitations of his subjects. Once, in the midst of this desolation, a single goat-herd, trusting to elude observation, disobeyed his prince's injunction, and pastured his flock in the luxuriant meadows of Ontála, on the banks of the Banás. After a few questions he was killed and hung up *in terrorem*. By such patriotic severity Partáp rendered the "garden of Rájasthán" of no value to the conqueror, and the

[1] A species of mimosa.

produce of European markets, already penetrating to the Mogul capital, was intercepted on its way from Súrat, and other ports, and plundered.

Akbar took the field against the Rájpút prince, establishing his headquarters at Ajmír. This celebrated fortress, destined ultimately to be one of the twenty-two *subahs* of the Mogul empire, had admitted for some time a royal garrison. Maldeo of Márwár, who had so ably opposed the usurper Sher Shah, was compelled to follow the example of his brother prince, Bhagwán Dás of Ambar, and to place himself at the footstool of Akbar. Only two years after Partáp's accession, after a brave but fruitless resistance in Mairtia and Jodhpúr, he sent his son, Udai Singh, to pay homage to the king. He was received with distinction at Nágor, and the title Rája was conferred upon him. Being of uncommon bulk, he was henceforth known as Mota Rája, or Udai *le gros*. He was the first of his race to give a daughter in marriage to the Tartar. The bribe for which he bartered his honour was splendid. Four new provinces, yielding £200,000 of annual revenue, were given in exchange for Jod Bai, the famous princess who became the mother of the emperor Shah Jahán, and whose magnificent tomb is still to be seen at Sikandra, not far from that in which Akbar's remains are deposited. With such examples as Márwár and Ambar, and with less power to resist the temptation, the minor chiefs of Rájasthán, with a brave and numerous vassalage, were transformed into satraps of Delhi, and in nearly every case their importance was increased by the change.

But these were fearful odds against Partáp. The arms of his country turned upon him, derived additional force from their self-degradation, which kindled into jealousy and hatred against the magnanimous resolution they lacked the virtue to imitate. When Hindu prejudice was thus violated by every prince in Rájasthán, the Rána renounced all alliance with those who were thus degraded. To the eternal honour of Partáp and his issue be it told that, to the very close of the monarchy of the Moguls, they refused such alliances not only with the throne, but even with their brother princes of Márwár and Ambar. It is a proud triumph of virtue to be able to record from the autograph letters of the most powerful of the Rájpút princes, Bukhet Singh and Jai Singh, that whilst they had risen to greatness by the surrender of principle, as Mewár had decayed from her adherence to it, they should solicit, and that humbly, to be readmitted to the honour of matrimonial intercourse—"to be purified," "to be regenerated," "to be made Rájpúts"—and that this favour was granted only on condition of their abjuring the contaminating practice which, for more than a century, had disunited them.

An anecdote illustrative of the settled repugnance of this noble family to sully the purity of its blood may here be related, as its result had a material influence on future events. Rája Mán, who had succeeded to the throne of Ambar, was the most celebrated of his race, and from him may be dated the rise of his country. He was also one of the first chiefs to sacrifice principle to expediency; and as Humáyun, as has already been related, espoused a daughter of Bhagwán Dás, he was the brother-in-law of Akbar. His courage and talents well seconded this advantage, and he became the first of the generals of the empire. To him Akbar was indebted for half his triumphs.

Rája Mán was returning from the conquest of Sholápúr to Hindustan when he invited himself to an interview with Partáp, then at Komulmír, who advanced to the Udai Ságar to receive him. On the mound which embanks this lake, a feast was prepared for the prince of Ambar. The board was spread, the Rája summoned, and prince Amra appointed to wait upon him; but no Rána appeared, for whose absence apologies alleging headache were urged by his son, with the request that Rája Mán would waive all ceremony, receive his welcome, and commence his repast. The prince in a tone at once dignified and respectful, replied: "Tell the Rána I can divine the cause of his headache; but the error is irremediable, and if he refuses to put a *khansa* before me, who will?" Further subterfuge was useless. The Rána appeared and expressed his regret; but added: "I cannot eat with a Rájpút who has given his daughter to a Toork, and who has probably eaten with him." Rája Mán was unwise to have risked this disgrace. He left the feast untouched, save for the few grains of rice he offered to Andeva, the god of food, observing as he withdrew, "It was for the preservation of your honour that we sacrificed our own, and gave our sisters and daughters to the Toork; but abide in peril, if such be your resolve, for this country shall not hold you," and, mounting his horse, he turned to the Rána and said: "If I do not humble your pride, my name is not Mán;" to which Partáp replied, "he should always be happy to meet him"; while some one, in less dignified terms, desired he would not forget to bring his *phúpa*,[1] Akbar The ground was deemed unclean where the feast had been spread: it was broken up and purified with water of the Ganges, and the chiefs who had witnessed the humiliation of one they deemed an apostate, bathed and changed their vestments. Every act was reported to the emperor, who was exasperated at the insult thus offered to himself; and the incident hastened the first of those sanguinary battles which have immortalised the name of Partáp.

Prince Salím, the heir of Delhi, led the war, guided by the counsels of Rája Mán and the distinguished apostate son of Ságarji, Muhabbat Khán. Partáp trusted to his native hills, and the valour of 22,000 Rájpúts to withstand the son of Akbar. The range to which he was restricted was the mountainous region around and chiefly to the west of the new capital. In length from north to south it was some eighty miles, and in breadth the same. The whole of this space is mountain and forest, valley and stream. The approaches to the fortress are defiles with lofty perpendicular rocks on either side, and so narrow that two carts can scarcely pass each other, but occasionally opening into spaces sufficiently capacious to encamp a whole army. Such a place was the plain of Haldighát, the scene of this bloody encounter, at the base of a *col*, or neck of mountain, which rendered it almost inaccessible. Above and below the Rájpúts were posted, and on the cliffs and pinnacles overlooking the field of battle were the faithful Bhíls, armed with their natural weapon, the bow and arrow, and with huge stones ready to roll down on the enemy.

[1] *I.e.*, uncle.

Partáp, with the flower of Mewár, defended the head of the pass, and glorious was the struggle for its maintenance. Clan after clan followed one another with desperate intrepidity, emulating the daring of their prince, who led the crimson banner into the hottest part of the field. In vain he strained every nerve to encounter Rája Mán; but though denied the luxury of revenge on his Rájpút foe, he made good a passage to where Salím commanded. The prince's guards fell before Partáp, and but for the steel plates which defended his *houdah*, the lance of the Rájpút would have deprived Akbar of his heir. His steed, the gallant Chituc, nobly seconded his lord, and is represented in all the historical drawings of this battle with one foot raised upon the elephant of the Mogul, while his rider has his lance propelled against his foe. The *mahárwat*, destitute of the means of defence, was slain, whereupon the infuriated animal, now without control, dashed away with his rider. On this spot the carnage was immense; the Moguls striving to defend Salím, and the heroes of Mewár to second their prince, who had already received seven wounds. Marked by the royal umbrella, which he would not lay aside, and which collected the might of the enemy against him, Partáp was thrice rescued from amidst the enemy, and was at length nearly overwhelmed, when Manah, the chief of Jhala, gave a signal instance of fidelity, and extricated him with the loss of his own life. Manah seized upon the insignia of Mewár, and, rearing the gold sun over his own head, drew after himself the brunt of the battle, while Partáp was forced from the field. The noble Jhala fell with all his brave vassals; and in remembrance of the deed, his descendants have, since the day of Haldighát, borne the regal ensigns of Mewar, and enjoyed "the right hand of her princes." But their valour was unavailing against a force which, besides being vastly superior in numbers, had the advantage of field artillery and a dromedary corps mounting swivels. Of Partáp's 22,000 warriors, only 8,000 quitted the field alive.

Unattended, the Rána fled on the gallant Chituc, who had borne him through the day, and who saved him now by leaping a mountain stream when closely pursued by two Mogul chiefs, whom this impediment momentarily checked. But Chituc, like his master, was wounded. Partáp's pursuers were gaining, the flash from the flinty rock announced them at his very heels, when there fell on his ear, in the broad accents of his native tongue, the salutation "*ho! níla ghora rá aswár!*" (ho! rider of the blue horse!) and, looking back, he beheld but a single horseman—that horseman his brother.

Sukta, whose personal enmity to Partáp had made him a traitor to Mewár, beheld from the ranks of Akbar the "blue horse" flying unattended. Resentment was extinguished, and a feeling of affection mingling with sad and humiliating recollections, took possession of his heart. He joined in the pursuit, but only to slay the pursuers, who fell beneath his lance; and now, for the first time in their lives, the two brothers embraced in friendship. Here, too, Chituc fell, and as the Rána unbuckled his caparison to place it upon Ankáro, presented to him by his brother, the noble steed expired. An altar was raised, and yet marks the spot where Chituc died; and the entire scene may be seen painted on the walls of half the houses of the capital.

The greeting between the princes was necessarily short, but Sukta quitted his brother with the assurance of reunion at the first safe opportunity. On rejoining Salím, the truth of his words was greatly doubted when he related that Partáp had not only slain his pursuers, but Ankáro as well. Salím pledged his word to spare him if he related the truth, and Sukta replied: "The burden of a kingdom is on my brother's shoulders, and I could not witness his danger without defending him." Salím kept his word, but dismissed the future head of the Suktáwats from his service. Sukta joined Partáp at Udaipúr. On his way thither, he captured Bhainsror. His brother made him a grant of the conquest, and it long remained the chief abode of his descendants.

Of the Rána's kin, 500 were slain in the battle of Haldighát. The ex-prince of Gwalior, with his son and 150 Tuár retainers paid the debt of gratitude with their lives. Since their expulsion by Bábar, they had found sanctuary in Mewár, whose princes diminished their feeble revenues to maintain inviolable the rites of hospitality. Manah lost 150 of his vassals, and every house of Mewár mourned its chief support.

Elate with victory, Salím left the hills. The rainy season had set in, which impeded operations, and obtained for Partáp a few months of repose; but with the spring the foe returned, and he was again defeated. He then took post in Komulmír, which was at once invested by Shábáz Khán. Here he made a gallant and protracted resistance, and did not retire till insects rendered the water of the

"Nogan" well, their sole resource, impure. This circumstance is imputed to the treachery of the Deora chief of Abu, who had gone over to Akbar. Partáp withdrew to Chaond, in the heart of the mountainous tract on the south-west of Mewár; while the Sonigura chief defended the place to the last. He was slain in the final assault, and by his side fell the chief bard of Mewár, who inspired by his deeds as well as by his song the spirit of resistance to the "ruthless king."

On the fall of Komulmír, the castle of Gogúnda was invested by Rája Mán. Muhammad Khán took possession of Udaipúr, and Faríd Khán approached Chaond from the south. Thus beset on every side, dislodged from his most secret retreats, and hunted from glen to glen, there appeared no hope for Partáp. Yet even whilst his pursuers deemed him panting in some obscure lurking place, he would, by mountain signals, reassemble his bands and assail them unawares. By a skilful movement, Faríd Khán was blocked up in a defile, and his force cut off to a man. The Moguls became weary of combating their ubiquitous enemy; and once more the monsoon, swelling the mountain streams, brought respite to Partap.

Years thus rolled away, each ending with a diminution of his means and an increase to his misfortunes. His family was his chief cause of anxiety; he dreaded their captivity—an apprehension often on the point of being realised. On one occasion they were saved by the faithful Bhíls, who carried them in wicker baskets and concealed them in the tin mines of Jaora, where they guarded and fed them. Bolts and rings are still preserved in the trees about Jaora and Chaond to which baskets, the only cradles of the royal children of Mewár, were suspended to preserve them from the tiger and the wolf. Yet amid such complicated evils, the fortitude of Partáp remained unshaken, and a spy sent by Akbar described how he saw the Rájpút and his chiefs seated at a scanty meal, maintaining all the etiquette observed in prosperity, the Rána bestowing the *dúnah* on the most deserving, which, though only of the fruits of the country, was received with all the reverence of better days.

But there were times when the wants of those dearer to him than his own life almost drove him to frenzy. His wife was insecure even in the mountain cave, and daily his children wept around him for food. Meals ready prepared had frequently to be abandoned for want of opportunity to eat them. Once his queen and his son's wife had prepared a few cakes from the flour of the meadow grass, of which one was given to each child; half for the present, the rest for a future meal. Partáp was stretched beside them pondering on his misfortunes, when a piercing cry from his daughter roused him from his reflections. A wild cat had darted on the reserved portion of the food, and the starving child shrieked with despair. Until that moment his fortitude had been unsubdued. He had beheld his sons and his kindred fall around him on the field without emotion—"for this the Rájpút was born"; but the lamentation of his children for food unmanned him. He cursed the name of royalty if only to be enjoyed on such conditions, and he demanded of Akbar a mitigation of his hardships.

Overjoyed at this indication of submission, the

emperor commanded public rejoicings, and exultingly showed the letter to Prithvi Ráj, a brother of the prince of Bíkanír, who had been compelled to follow the victorious car of Akbar. The state of Bíkanír had recently grown out of the Rahtors of Márwár, and, being exposed on the flats of the desert, had been able to offer but little resistance. Prithvi Ráj was one of the most gallant cavaliers of the age, and, like the Troubadour princes of the west,[1] he could grace a cause with elegant verse as well as aid it with the sword: indeed, in an assembly of the bards of Rájasthán, the palm of merit was unanimously awarded to the Rahtor cavalier. He adored the very name of Partáp, and Akbar's intelligence filled him with grief. With all the warmth and frankness of his nature, he told the king that the letter was the forgery of some foe to the fame of the Rájpút prince. "I know him well," he said; "for your crown he would not submit to your terms." He requested and obtained permission to transmit by his courier a letter to Partáp, ostensibly to ascertain the fact of his submission, but in reality with a view to prevent it. The stirring couplets which composed the missive were to the following effect: "The hopes of the Hindu rest on the Hindu; yet the Rána forsakes them. But for Partáp, all would be placed on the same level by Akbar; for our chiefs have lost their valour and our females their honour. Akbar is the broker in the market of our race: all has he purchased but the son of Udai; he is beyond his price. Despair has driven many to this mart to witness their dishonour: from such infamy the descendant of Hamír alone has been preserved. The world asks, whence the concealed aid of Partáp? He has no aïd but the soul of manliness and his sword; with them well has he maintained the *khatri's*[1] pride. This broker in the market of men will one day be overreached; he cannot live for ever:. then will our race come to Partáp for the seed of the Rájpút to sow in our desolate fields. To him all look for its preservation, that its purity may again become resplendent."

This effusion of the Rahtor was equal to 10,000 men; it nerved the drooping mind of Partáp, and roused him into action, for it was a noble incentive to find every eye of his race fixed upon him. Unable any longer to hold his own in Mewár, he determined to lead his Sesodias to the Indus, plant the crimson banner on the insular capital of the Sogdi, and leave a desert between himself and his inexorable foe. With his family and all that was yet noble in Mewár, he descended the Arávalli, and had reached the confines of the desert when an incident occurred which caused him to change his plans, and to continue a dweller in the land of his forefathers. To Bhama Sah belongs the honour of having saved his country at this critical juncture. He was the Rána's minister—an office which had long been hereditary in his family; and he now offered to his master the accumulated wealth of himself and his ancestors, which, with other resources, is stated to have been sufficient for the maintenance of 25,000 men for twelve years. This magnificent offering enabled Partáp once more to collect his bands; and, while his foes imagined that he was endeavouring to effect a retreat through the

[1] The *khatri* is the same as the *kshatriya*, the second of the four grand Hindu castes.

desert, he fell suddenly on Shábáz in his camp at Deweir and cut his troops to pieces. The fugitives were pursued to Amait, whose garrison suffered the same fate. Ere the royal forces could recover from their consternation at this astonishing resurrection, Komulmír was assaulted and taken; Abdulla and his garrison were put to the sword, and thirty-two other fortified posts were carried by surprise, the troops being put to death without mercy. In one short campaign, Partáp recovered the whole of Mewár, except Chítor, Ajmír, and Mandalgarh; and as some slight return to Rája Mán, who had fulfilled to the letter his threat that Partáp should "live in peril," he invaded Ambar, and sacked its chief mart of commerce, Malpúra.

Udaipúr was also regained, though this acquisition was so unimportant as scarcely to merit remark. In all likelihood it was abandoned by Akbar from the difficulty of defending it when all around had submitted to Partáp, though the annals ascribe the event to a generous sentiment of the emperor, prompted by his great *khánkhánan*, Abul Fázil, whose mind appears to have been captivated by the actions of the Rájpút prince. For the repose which he enjoyed during the latter years of his life, Partáp was indebted to a combination of causes. In the main it is to be attributed to the fact that Akbar had found new fields for his ambition in the south, though full weight must also be given to the influence which the conduct of the Hindu prince had exerted, not only upon Akbar, but upon the many Rájpút princes who swelled his train, and whose inclinations it would have been dangerous to treat with indifference.

Repose was, however, no boon to Partáp. A mind

Photo by] *Donald Macbeth, London*

COLUMNS IN THE FORTRESS OF CHÍTOR.

[*p.* 94

such as his could enjoy no tranquillity while, from the summit of the pass which guarded Udaipúr, his eye embraced the *kangras* of Chítor, to which he knew that he must ever be a stranger. Burning for the redemption of the glory of his race, the mercy thus shown to him was more difficult of endurance than the pangs of Tantalus. Imagine the warrior, yet in manhood's prime, broken with fatigue and covered with scars, casting a wistful eye to the rock stained with the blood of his fathers, whilst in the "dark chamber" of his mind the scenes of glory enacted there appeared with unearthly lustre. First the youthful Bappa, on whose head was the "*mor* he had won from the Mori"; next, the warlike Samársi, arming for the last day of Rájpút independence, to die with Prithvi Ráj on the banks of the Caggar. Again, descending the steep of Chítor, the twelve sons of Arsi, the crimson banner floating around each, while from the embattled rock the guardian goddess looks down on the carnage which is to secure a perpetuity of sway. Again, in all the pomp of sacrifice the Deola chief, succeeded in turn by Jaimal and Patta, and, like the Pallas of Rájasthán, the Chondáwat dame leading her daughter into the ranks of destruction; and at last clouds of darkness dim the walls of Chítor and out of them Udai Singh appears flying from the rock to which the honour of the house is united.

Aghast at the picture his mind had portrayed, imagine him turning to contemplate his own condition, indebted for a cessation of persecution to the most revolting sentiment that can assail an heroic mind—compassion, compared with which scorn is endurable, contempt even enviable. These he could retaliate, but for the high-minded, the generous Rájpút, to be the object of that sickly sentiment, pity, was more oppressive than the arms of his foe. A premature decay assailed the pride of Rájasthán; a mind diseased prayed on an exhausted frame, and prostrated him in the very summer of his days. The last moments of Partáp were an appropriate commentary on his life, which he terminated like the Carthagenian, swearing his successor to eternal conflict with the enemies of his country's independence.

A powerful sympathy is excited by the picture which is drawn of this last scene. The dying hero is represented in a lowly dwelling; his chiefs—the faithful companions of many a glorious day—await round his pallet the dissolution of their prince. A groan of mental anguish makes Salúmbra enquire what afflicts his soul that it cannot depart in peace. "It lingers," is the reply, "for some consolatory pledge that my country shall not be abandoned to the Toork;" and with the death pang on him, he relates an incident which had guided his estimate of his son's disposition, and led him to fear that, for personal ease, he would forego the remembrance of his own and his country's wrongs. On the banks of the Peshoda, he tells them, he and his men had constructed a few huts to protect them from the inclemency of the rains in the days of their distress. Prince Amra forgot the lowliness of the dwelling, and a projecting bamboo of the roof caught the folds of his turban and dragged it off as he entered. A hasty ejaculation disclosed his annoyance, and Partáp, observing it, formed the opinion that his son would never withstand the hardships to be endured in their cause. "These sheds," said the dying prince, "will give way to sumptuous dwellings, thus generating the love of ease; and the independence of Mewár, which we have bled to maintain, will be sacrificed to luxury. And you, my chiefs," he added, "will follow the pernicious example." They pledged themselves, and became guarantees for the prince, "by the throne of Bappa Ráwul," that they would not permit mansions to be raised till Mewár had recovered her independence; and then the soul of Partáp was satisfied, and he expired in peace.

Thus closed the life of a Rájpút whose memory is even now idolised by every Sesodia, and will continue to be so, till renewed oppression shall extinguish the remaining sparks of patriotic feeling. It is worthy the attention of those who influence the destinies of states in more favoured climes to estimate the intensity of feeling which could arm this prince to oppose the resources of a small principality against what was at that time one of the most powerful empires of the world, whose armies were more numerous and far more efficient than any ever led by the Persian against the liberties of Greece. Had Mewár possessed her Thucydides or her Xenophon, neither the wars of the Peloponesus nor the retreat of the "ten thousand" would have yielded more diversified incidents for the historic muse than the deeds of this brilliant reign. Undaunted heroism, inflexible fortitude, perseverance which "keeps honour bright," with fidelity such as no other nation can boast, were the materials opposed to soaring ambition, commanding talents, unlimited means, and the fervour of religious zeal; all, however, insufficient to contend with one unconquerable mind. There is not a pass in the Alpine Arávalli that is not sanctified by some deed of Partáp—some brilliant victory or more glorious defeat. Haldighát is the Thermopylae of Mewár: the field of Deweir is her Marathon.

ix.—Rána Amra Singh

Of the seventeen sons of Partáp, Amra, who succeeded him, was the eldest. From the early age of eight he had been his father's constant companion, and the partner of his toils and dangers. Instructed in every act of mountain strife, and familiar with its perils, he entered on his career in the very flower of manhood, already attended by sons able to maintain whatever his sword might recover of his patrimony. Akbar survived Partáp nearly eight years. The vast field in which he had now to exert the resources of his mind necessarily withdrew him from a scene where even success ill repaid the sacrifices made to attain it, and Amra was left in complete repose during the remainder of this monarch's life. An extended reign of more than half a century enabled the Mogul to consolidate the vast empire he had erected, while the form of government which he established affords incontestible proof both of his genius and his natural benevolence. It is a proud tribute to the memory of Akbar that his name is united with that of his rival Partáp in numerous traditionary couplets honourable to both; and if the Rájpút bard naturally emblazons first on his page the virtues of his own hero, he admits that none other but Akbar can stand comparison with him; thereby confirming the eulogy of the imperial historian who observes, in summing up his master's character, that "if he sometimes did things beneath the dignity of a great king, he never did anything unworthy of a good man."

Amra remodelled the institutions of his country, made a new assessment of the lands and distribution of the fiefs, established the gradation of ranks as it now exists, and regulated the sumptuary laws even to the tie of a turban. Many of these laws are to be seen engraved on pillars of stone in various parts of the country. But the repose he enjoyed was not without its dangers, and at one time seemed likely to bring about the realisation of his father's prophetic fears. Amra constructed for himself a palace on the banks of the lake, named after himself the "abode of immortality," remarkable for its Gothic contrast to the splendid marble edifice erected by his predecessors, and now the abode of the princes of Mewár, yet a residence by no means devoid of stately luxury, and one ill calculated to foster the memory of his father's admonitions.

Jahángír having been four years on the throne, and, having overcome all internal dissensions, resolved to signalise his reign by the subjugation of the only prince who had disdained to acknowledge the paramount power of the Moguls. Amra, between the love of ease and reputation, wavered as to the course he should adopt; nor were sycophants wanting who

> Counselled ignoble ease and peaceful sloth,
> Not peace:

and dared to prompt his following the universal contagion by accepting the imperial firman. In such a state of mind the chiefs found him when they went to his new abode to warn him to prepare for the emergency. The gallant Chondáwats, recalling the dying behest of their late prince, demanded its fulfilment; and urged every argument their patriotism could devise to rouse their apathetic leader to action.

A magnificent mirror of European manufacture adorned the embryo palace. Animated with a noble resentment at the inefficacy of his appeal to the better feelings of his prince, the chieftain of Salumbra hurled the "slave of the carpet"[1] against the splendid bauble, and, starting up, seized his sovereign by the arm and moved him from his throne. "To horse, chiefs!" he exclaimed, "and preserve from infamy the son of Partáp." A burst of anger followed the seeming indignity, and the patriot was branded with the harsh name of traitor; but with his sacred duty in view, and supported by every vassal of note, he calmly disregarded the insult. Compelled to mount his horse, and surrounded by the veterans of all the chivalry of Mewár, Amra's passion vented itself in tears of indignation. In such a mood the cavalcade descended the ridge, and had reached the spot where the temple of Jaggarnáth now stands, when the prince recovered from his fit of passion—the tears ceased to flow, and, making a courteous salutation, he entreated forgiveness for his omission of respect; and more especially expressing his gratitude to Salumbra, he said: "Lead on, nor shall you ever have to regret your late sovereign." Elevated with every sentiment of generosity and valour, they passed on to Dewier, where they encountered the royal army, led by the brother of the Khánkhánan, as it entered the pass, and, after a long and sanguinary combat, gained a complete victory.

The honours of the day are chiefly attributed to

[1] A brass weight placed on the corner of a carpet.

the brave Kana, uncle of the Rána, and ancestor of the numerous clan called after him the Kanáwats. A truce followed this battle, but it was of short duration, for another and yet more murderous conflict took place in the spring of 1606, in the pass of Rampúr, where the imperial army, under its leader Abdulla, was almost exterminated, though with the loss of the best and bravest of the Sesodia chiefs. A feverish exultation was the fruit of this victory, which shed a hectic flush of glory over the declining days of Mewár, when the crimson banner once more floated throughout the province of Godwár.

Alarmed at these successive defeats, Jahángír, preparatory to equipping a fresh army, determined to establish a new Rána, and to instal him in the ancient seat of power, Chítor, hoping thus to withdraw from the standard of Amra many of his adherents. The experiment evinced at least a knowledge of their prejudices; but, to the honour of Rájpút fidelity, it failed. Sugra, who abandoned Partáp and went over to Akbar, was selected; the sword of sovereignty was girded on him by the emperor's own hands; and, under the escort of a Mogul force, he took possession of his ruined capital. For seven years Sugra had a spurious homage paid to him. But it is gratifying to record that not even by this recreant son of Chítor could the impressions formed in contemplating the scenes around him be resisted; and Sugra, though flinty as the rock to a brother and a nephew, was unable to support the silent rebuke of the altars of the heroes of his race, and, at length, sending for Amra, he handed over to him Chítor, and himself retired to Rinthambúr. Some time after, upon going to court, and being upbraided by Jahángír, he drew his dagger and slew himself in the emperor's presence—an end worthy of such a traitor.

Amra took possession of the seat of his ancestors; but wanting the means to put it in defence, the acquisition did little more than increase the temporary exultation. With Chítor the Rána acquired, by surrender or assault, possession of no less than eighty of the chief towns and fortresses of Mewár, amongst them being Ontála, the siege of which is famous for one of the most extraordinary exhibitions of Rájpút courage recorded in the annals of Rájasthán. The right to lead the *herole* (vanguard), which had for generations belonged to the Chondáwats, was on this occasion disputed by the Suktáwats, whose well-known valour went far to justify their claim. The sword would have decided the matter, but for the tact of the prince. "The *herole* to the clan which first enters Ontála" was his decision, which was readily accepted by the Suktáwats, while their rivals could no longer plead their right when such a gauntlet was thrown down for its maintenance.

Ontála is about eighteen miles east of Udaipúr, commanding the road leading to the ancient capital. It is situated on rising ground, with a stream flowing beneath its walls, which are of solid masonry, lofty, and with round towers at intervals. In the centre was the Governor's house, also fortified. The stronghold could be entered but by a single gateway. The clans moved off at the same time, some hours before dawn—Ontála the goal, the *herole* the reward. The Suktáwats made directly for the gateway, which they reached as the day broke. The foe were taken by surprise, but the walls were soon manned and the action commenced. The Chondáwats, less skilled in topography, had traversed a swamp which retarded them, but through which they dashed, fortunately meeting a guide in a shepherd of Ontála. With more foresight than their rivals, they had brought ladders. The chief led the escalade, but a ball rolled him back amidst his vassals. The next in rank and kin took the command. He was one of those arrogant, reckless Rájpúts, who signalised themselves wherever there was danger, and his common appellation was the "Benda Thákúr," or the "mad chief" of Deogarh. When his leader fell, he rolled the body in his scarf; then, tying it on his back, scaled the wall, and having cleared the way before him with his lance, he threw it over the parapet of Ontála, shouting, "The vanguard to the Chondáwat! we are first in!" Meanwhile, the Suktáwat, depending on the elephant he rode, was trying to force the gate, but its projecting spikes deterred the animal from applying his strength. His men were falling thick around him, and a shout from the other party made him dread their success. He descended from his seat, placed his body on the spikes, and commanded the driver, on pain of instant death, to propel the elephant against him. The gates gave way, and over the body of their chief, his clan rushed into the fortress with the victorious cry of the Chondáwats ringing in their ears. The Mogul garrison was overpowered and put to the sword; the standard of Mewár waved over the castle; but the leading of the vanguard remained with the descendants of Chonda.

It will not be unfitting if we here give some account of the rise of the Suktáwats, with whom is materially connected the future history of Mewár. Sukta was the second of the twenty-four sons of Udai Singh. When only five years of age, he discovered that fearless temperament which marked his manhood. The armourer having brought a new dagger to try its edge by the usual proof on thinly-spread cotton, the child asked the Rána "if it was not meant to cut flesh and bones," and seizing it tried it on his own little hand. The blood gushed on the carpet, but he betrayed no symptom of pain or surprise. His father, recalling, perhaps, the prediction of the astrologers, who, in casting Sukta's horoscope, had announced that he was to be the "bane of Mewár," forthwith commanded that he should be put to death. The child was carried off for the purpose, but was saved, by the Salumbra chief, who arrested the fiat, sped to the Rána, and begged his life as a boon, promising, having no heirs, to educate him as the future head of the Chondáwats. The chief had children in his old age, and while he was wavering between the child of his adoption and his own issue, the young Sukta was sent for to court by his brother Partáp. For some time the two brothers lived together on the most amicable footing; but one day whilst hunting a dispute arose which grew so bitter that Partáp suggested that they should decide it by single combat. Sukta was nothing loth; but as they took their ground and were about to charge together, the *purohit* rushed between them, and implored them not to bring ruin on their house. His appeal being in vain, the priest saw but one way to prevent the unnatural strife. He drew his dagger, and, plunging it into his breast, fell a lifeless corpse between the combatants. Appalled at the horrid deed, "the blood of a priest on their heads," they desisted from their infatuated aim. Partáp, waving his hand, commanded Sukta to quit his dominions; and the latter, his pride unsubdued, carried his resentment to Akbar. Partáp performed with the obsequies of his faithful servant many expiatory rites, and made an irrevocable grant of Salaira to his son, which is still enjoyed by his descendants, while a small column yet identifies the spot of sacrifice to fidelity. Sukta and Partáp never saw each other again until their romantic meeting after the battle of Haldighát.

Sukta had seventeen sons, all of whom, excepting the heir of Bhainsror,[1] attended his obsequies. On their return from this rite, they found the gates barred against them by Bhanji, now chief of the Suktáwats, who told them there were "too many mouths in Bhainsror" and that they must push their fortunes elsewhere; so, demanding their arms and their horses, they departed to seek a new home. After many wanderings and vicissitudes, they were summoned to the assistance of Amra at Ontála, where their brother joined them, and where they won undying fame for their clan in the manner already described. Bhanji soon afterwards performed a service which obtained for him the entire favour of his prince. The latter was insulted by the Rahtors of Bhíndír, whereupon Bhanji marched against their town, and took it by assault. Amra added it to his fief, and Bhíndír instead of Bhainsror became the abode of the clan. Ten chiefs followed in regular succession, and a few

[1] *See* p. 89.

generations after Sukta the clan could muster 10,000 men.

Jahángír, being by this time thoroughly alarmed, determined to equip an overwhelming force to crush the Rána. To this end he raised the imperial standard at Ajmír, and assembled the expedition under his own immediate inspection. He appointed his son Parvez commander, with instructions on departure "that if the Rána or his eldest son Kurran should repair to him, to receive them with becoming attention, and to offer no molestation to the country." But the Sesodia prince little thought of submission: on the contrary, flushed with success, he met the royal army at a spot oft moistened with blood, the pass of Khamnor, leading into the heart of the hills. The imperialists were disgracefully defeated, and fled, pursued with great slaughter to Ajmír. The Mogul historian admits it to have been a glorious day for Mewár. He describes Parvez entangled in the passes, dissensions in his camp, and his supplies cut off; and refers to "his precipitate flight and pursuit, in which the royal army lost vast numbers of men." But Jahángír, in his diary, slurs over the affair, and simply remarks: "I recalled Parvez to rejoin me at Lahore, and directed his son with some chiefs to be left to watch the Rána."

This son, tutored by the great Muhabbat Khán, fared no better than Parvez; he was routed and slain. But the Hydra was indestructible; and every victory, while it cost the best blood of Mewár, only multiplied the number of her foes. Seventeen pitched battles had the illustrious Rájpút fought since the death of his father; but the loss of his experienced veterans withered the laurels of victory, nor had he sufficient repose either to husband his forces, or to rear his young heroes to replace their dead sires. Another and yet mightier army was assembled under Prince Khuram, the ablest of the sons of Jáhángír, and better known in history as the emperor Shah Jahán. Again did the Rána with his son Kurran collect the might of the hills; but a handful of warriors was all their muster to meet the host of Delhi, and the "crimson banner" which for more than eight hundred years had waved in proud independence over the heads of the Gehlotes, was now to be abased to the son of Jahángír. The emperor's own pen shall narrate the termination of this strife.

"The eighth year of my reign, I determined to move to Ajmír, and to send my fortunate son Khuram before me; and having fixed the moment of departure I despatched him with magnificent *khilats*, an elephant, horse, sword, shield, and dagger, and besides his usual force, I added 12,000 horse under Azím Khán, and presented to all the officers of his army suitable gratifications.

"In the ninth year of my reign, while seated on my throne, in an auspicious moment, the elephant Alam Goman, with seventeen others, male and female, captured from the Rána, were sent by my son and presented to me. The next day I went abroad mounted on Alam Goman, to my great satisfaction, and distributed gold in great quantity.

"Pleasing intelligence arrived of the intention of Rána Amra Singh to repair and make his obeisance to me. My fortunate son had established my authority and garrisons in divers strongholds of the Rána's country, which, owing to the malign influence of the water and the air, its barrenness

Photo by] [*Donald Macbeth, London*

THE FORTRESS OF AJMÍR.

and inaccessibility, it was deemed impossible to bring under subjection; yet from the perpetual over-running of the country by my armies, without regard to the heat or the rains, and the capture and imprisonment of the wives and children of many of the men of rank of the country, the Rána was at length reduced to acknowledge the despair to which he was driven, and that a further continuance of such distress would be attended with utter ruin, with the choice of captivity, or of being forced to abandon his country. He, therefore, determined to make his submission, and sent two of his chiefs, Supkuran and Heridás, to my son Khuram, to represent that if he would forgive, and take him by the hand, he would pay his respects to him, and would send his eldest son Kurran to attend and serve the emperor, as did other Hindu princes; but that on account of his years, he would hold himself excused from attending in person.

"I was greatly rejoiced at this event happening under my own reign, and I commanded that these, the ancient possessors of the country, should not be driven from it. The fact is that the Rána Amra Singh and his ancestors were proud, and confident in the strength and inaccessibility of their mountainous country and its strongholds, and had never beheld a king of Hindustan, nor made obeisance to one. I was desirous, in my own fortunate time, that the opportunity should not slip my hands; instantly, therefore, on the representation of my son, I forgave the Rána, and sent a friendly firman that he might rest assured of my protection and care, and imprinted thereon, as a solemn testimony of my sincerity, my 'five fingers'; I also wrote to my son that, by any means by which it could be brought about, to treat this illustrious one according to his own heart's wishes. My son despatched the firman by the chiefs Supkuran and Heridás, with assurances to the Rána that he might rely on my generosity and esteem; and it was agreed that on the 28th of the month he should repair to my son.

"Having gone to Ajmír to hunt, Mahmúd Beg, a servant of my son Khuram, arrived and presented a letter from him, and stated to me verbally that the Rána had met my son. On receiving this news, I presented Mahmúd Beg with an elephant, horse, and dagger, and gave him the title of Zulfikar Khán.

"The Rána, with due attention to etiquette, as other vassals of the empire, paid his respects to my son, and presented him with a celebrated ruby, and various arms inlaid with gold, seven elephants of great price, which had remained after those previously captured, and nine horses. My son received him with princely generosity and courtesy, and the Rána, taking him by the knee, requested to be forgiven. My son raised him, and gave him every assurance of countenance and protection, and presented him with suitable *khilats*, an elephant, horses, and a sword. Though he had not one hundred persons in his train worthy to be dignified with *khilats*, yet 120 *khilats*, 50 horses, and 12 jewelled aigrettes were bestowed upon them. The custom, however, of these princes being that the heir and the father never visit together, he observed this usage, and Kurran, his declared successor, did not accompany the Rána. Sultán Khuram, the same day, gave Amra Singh his leave, and forthwith the son arrived; whereupon Sultán Khuram repaired with him to me.

"In my interview with Sultán Khuram on his arrival at Ajmír, he represented that if it was my pleasure, he would present the prince Kurran to me, whom I accordingly desired him to bring. He arrived and paid his respects, and his rank was commanded to be, at the request of my son, immediately on my right hand. As Kurran, owing to the rude life he had led in his natives hills, was extremely shy, and unused to the pageantry and experience of a court, in order to reconcile him and give him confidence, I daily gave him some testimony of my regard and protection, and on the second day of his service, I gave him a jewelled dagger, and on the third a choice steed of Irák with rich caparison; and on the same day I took him with me to the queen's court, when the queen, Núr Jahán, presented him with a splendid *khilat*, elephant and horse caparisoned, sword, etc. I gave him three royal hawks, and three falcons trained to the hand, a coat of mail, chain and plate armour, and two rings of value; and on the last day of the month, carpets, state cushions, perfumes, vessels of gold, and a pair of the bullocks of Gujarát.

"In the tenth year of my reign, I gave prince Kurran leave to depart; when I bestowed upon him an elephant, a horse, a pearl necklace valued at 50,000 rupees (£6250). From the day of his repairing to my court to that of his departure, the value of the gifts I presented to him exceeded 10 lakhs of rupees (£125,000), exclusive of 110 horses, 5 elephants, and the gifts of my son

Khuram. I sent Mubárak Khán along with him, who carried for me various confidential messages to the Rána. In the same year of my reign, Jaggat Singh, son of Kurran, aged twelve years, arrived at my court, and paid his respects, and presented the *arzís* (petitions) of his father and grandfather. His countenance carried the impression of his illustrious extraction, and I delighted his heart with presents and kindness. At his departure, I presented him with 20,000 rupees, a horse, elephant, and *khilat*; and to Heridás, his preceptor, 5,000 rupees, a horse, and *khilat*.

"In the eleventh year of my reign, statues of the Rána and Kurran were sculptured in white marble, and I commanded that they should be placed in the gardens at Agra. The same year I received intimation that Sultán Khuram had entered the territory of the Rána, and had exchanged visits with him and his son; and that from the tribute, consisting of seven elephants, twenty-seven saddle horses, trays of jewels, and ornaments of gold, my son took three horses, and returned all the rest, and engaged that prince Kurran and 1500 Rájpút horse should remain with him in the wars.

"In the thirteenth year of my reign, prince Kurran repaired to my court at Sindla, to congratulate me on my victories and the conquest of the Dekhan, and presented 100 gold mohurs, 1000 rupees, and gold ornaments and jewels to the value of 21,000 rupees.

"In the fourteenth year of my reign, I received intelligence of the death of Rána Amra Singh. To Bhím Singh his son, and Jaggat Singh his grandson, who were in attendance on me, I gave *khilats*;

and I despatched Rája Kishore Dás with a firman conferring benefits and the dignity of Rána on prince Kurran, the *khilat* being accompanied by the robe of investiture, choice horses, and a letter of condolence suitable to the occasion. In the firman, I expressed to Rána Kurran my desire that his son, with his contingent, should attend me."

To have generalised the details of the royal historian would have been to lessen the interest of this important period in the annals of Mewár. Jahángír merits to have his exultation described by his own pen. With his self-gratulation, he bears full testimony to the gallant and long-protracted resistance of the Rájpút; and while he impartially, though rather erroneously, estimates their motives and means of opposition, he does Amra ample justice in the declaration that he did not yield until he had but the alternative of captivity or exile; and with a magnanimity above all praise, he records the Rájpút prince's salvo for his dignity, "that he would hold himself excused from attending the emperor in person." The simple and naïve declaration of his joy, his "going abroad" on Alam Goman on hearing of the Rána's submission, is far more effective than the most pompous description of public rejoicing. But there is a heart-stirring philanthropy in the conduct of the Mogul which does him immortal honour; and in commanding his son "to treat the illustrious one according to his heart's wishes," though he had so long and so signally foiled the royal armies, he proved himself worthy of the good fortune he acknowledges, and well shows his sense of the superiority of the chief of all the Rájpúts by placing the heir of Mewár even above the princes of his own house, immediately "on his right hand." Whether attempting to relieve the shyness of Kurran, or to set forth the princely appearance of Jaggat Singh, we see the same amiable feeling operating to lighten the chains of the conquered. But the shyness of Kurran deserves a nobler term; he felt the degradation which neither the statues raised to them, the right hand of the monarch, the dignity of a "commander of five thousand," nor even the restoration of the long-alienated territory, could neutralise, when the kingdom to which he was heir was called a fief, and himself, the descendant of a hundred kings, the vassal of the empire, under whose banner, which his ancestors had so courageously opposed, he was now to follow with a contingent of 1500 Rájpút horse.

Seldom has subjugated authority met with such consideration; yet, to a lofty mind like Amra's, this conscious condescension but increased the severity of endurance. In the bitterness of his heart, he cursed the magnanimity of Khuram, whose Rájpút descent and sympathies, more than the force of arms, had induced him to surrender; for Khuram asked but the friendship of the Rájpút as the price of peace, and agreed to withdraw every Muhammadan from Mewár if the Rána would consent to receive the emperor's firman outside the walls of his capital. This his proud soul rejected, and though he visited Prince Khuram as a friend, he spurned the proposition of acknowledging a superior, or receiving the rank and titles awaiting such an admission. The noble Amra, who

> . . . rather than be less,
> Preferred not to be at all,

took the resolution to abdicate the throne he could no longer hold but at the will of another. Assembling his chiefs, and disclosing his determination, he made the *tíka* on his son's forehead, and, observing that the honour of Mewár was now in his hands, forthwith left the capital, and secluded himself in the Nauchoki, nor did he from that hour cross its threshold but to have his ashes deposited with those of his fathers.

All comment is superfluous on such a character as that of Rána Amra. He was worthy of Partáp and his race. He possessed the physical as well as the mental qualities of a hero, and was the tallest and strongest of all the princes of Mewár. He was not so fair as others of his race, and he had a reserve bordering on gloominess, doubtless occasioned by his reverses, for it was not natural to him or to his family. He was beloved by his chiefs for the qualities they most esteemed, generosity and valour, and by his subjects for his justice and charity, of which we can judge from his edicts, many of which yet live on the column or the rock.

x.—Jaggat Singh and Ráj Singh

KURRAN succeeded the last independent king of Mewár in 1621. Henceforth we shall have to exhibit these princely "children of the sun" with diminished lustre, moving as satelites round the primary planet. Unaccustomed to the laws of its attraction, they frequently deviated from the orbit prescribed, and in the eccentricity of their movements occasionally displayed their unborrowed effulgence. For fifteen hundred years we have traced each alteration in the fortunes of the Sesodias—their establishment in Suráshtra and expulsion therefrom by the Parthians, the acquisition and loss of Idar, the conquest and surrender of Chítor, the rise of Udaipúr, and, finally, the abasement of the red flag to Jahángír. The remaining, and by no means least important, portion of their history will conclude with the unity of their interests with those of Great Britain.

Kurran was deficient neither in courage nor military skill; of both he had given a decided proof when, to relieve the pecuniary difficulties of his father, he passed through the midst of his foes, surprised and plundered Súrat, and carried off a booty which was the means of postponing the subjugation of his country. But, for the exercise of the chief virtue of the Rájpút, he had little opportunity throughout his reign, and fortunately for Mewár the powerful esteem which Jahángír and Prince Khuram evinced for his house enabled him to put forth the talents he possessed to repair her distress. He fortified the heights round the capital, which he strengthened with a wall and a ditch, enlarged the noble dam which retains the waters of the Peshola, and built that entire portion of the palace called the *ráwula* still set apart for the ladies of the court.

When Rána Amra made terms with Jahángír, he obtained for his successors exemption from all personal attendance at the court, and confined the extent of homage to their receiving, on each lapse of the crown, the firman or imperial decree in token of subordination, which, more strongly to mark their dependent position, the Rána was to accept without the walls of the capital. Hence, though the princes of Mewár attended the emperor whilst heirs-apparent, they never did so as Ránas.

The Sesodia chieftains were soon distinguished amongst the Rájpút vassals of the Mogul, and had a full share of power. Of these Bhím, the younger brother of Kurran, and leader of the Mewár contingent, was conspicuous, and became the chief adviser and friend of Khuram, who well knew his intrepidity. At his son's solicitation, the emperor conferred upon him the title of Rája, and assigned a small estate on the banks of the Banás for his residence. Ambitious of perpetuating his name, he erected a new city and palace which he named Rájmahal, and which remained in the possession of his descendants for many generations. The ruins of Rájmahal bear testimony to the architectural taste of this son of Mewár, as do the fallen fortunes of his house to the instability of power.

Notwithstanding these favours, Jahángír soon had a specimen of the insubordinate spirit of Bhím.

Being desirous to separate him from Prince Khuram, who aspired to the crown, to the prejudice of his elder brother Parvez, he appointed him to the government of Gujarát, but Bhím boldly declined to accept the post. He detested Parvez, who, it will be remembered, had invaded Mewár, and advised Khuram, if he aspired to reign, to throw off the mask. The result was that Parvez was slain, and Khuram manifested his guilt by taking to arms. He was secretly supported by a strong party of the Rájpút interest, at the head of which was Gaj Singh of Márwár, his maternal uncle, who, pending the development of events, assumed an attitude of neutrality. Jahángír advanced to crush the incipient revolt; but, distrusting Gaj Singh, he gave the command to Jaipúr, and the former furled his banner and decided to be a spectator. The armies approached and were joining action when the impetuous Bhím sent a message to the Rahtor, either to aid or oppose them. The insult provoked him to the latter course, and Bhím's party was destroyed, himself slain, and Khuram and Muhabbat Khán compelled to take refuge in Udaipúr.

In this asylum the Mogul prince remained undisturbed. Apartments in the palace were assigned to him; but, his followers showed so little respect for Rájpút prejudices that he took up his abode on the island, on which a sumptuous residence was raised, adorned with a lofty dome and crowned with a crescent. The interior was decorated with onyx, cornelean, jasper, and agates, and the floors were covered with rich Turkey carpets. Here Khuram resided, every wish anticipated, till a short time before the death of his father, when he retired to Persia.

Photo by] [*Donald Macbeth, London*

RÁJMAHAL.
On the Banás River.

[*p.* 118

Such was Rájpút gratitude to a prince who, when the chances of war made him victor over them, had sought unceasingly to mitigate the misery attendant on the loss of independence; and, though two centuries have fled, during which Mewár has suffered every variety of woe, pillaged by Mogul, Pathán, and Mahrátta, yet the turban of prince Khuram, the symbol of fraternity,[1] has been preserved, and remains in the same folds as when transferred from the head of the Mogul to that of the Rájpút prince.

Rána Kurran had enjoyed eight years of complete tranquillity when he was gathered to his fathers. The sanctuary he gave Prince Khuram had no apparent effect on Jahángír, who, doubtless, believed that the Rána disapproved of the conduct of his son Bhím. He was succeeded by Jaggat Singh in 1628. Jahángír died shortly after Jaggat's accession, and while Khuram was in exile. This event was announced to the latter by the Rána, who sent his brother and a band of Rájpúts to Súrat to form the escort of the new emperor, who repaired directly to Udaipúr; and it was in the Bádal Mahal of his island palace that he was first saluted by the title Shah Jahán. On taking leave, he restored to Mewár five alienated districts, and presented the Rána with a ruby of inestimable value, giving him also permission to reconstruct the fortifications of Chítor.

The twenty-six years during which Jaggat Singh occupied the throne passed in uninterrupted peace —a state unfruitful to the bard, who flourishes only amidst agitation and strife. This period was devoted to the cultivation of the peaceful arts, and especially architecture; and to Jaggat Singh Udaipúr is

[1] An exchange of turbans is the symbol of fraternal adoption.

indebted for those magnificent works which bear his name, and excite our astonishment at the resources he found to accomplish them. The palace on the lake, called the Jagnewás, which covers four acres, is entirely his work, as well as the Jagmandar palace and many other buildings on the same island. Nothing but marble enters into their composition; columns, baths, reservoirs, fountains, all are of this material, often inlaid with mosaics, the uniformity pleasingly diversified by the light passing through coloured glass. The walls, both here and in the grand palace, contain many medallions in gypsum, portraying the chief events in the history of the family. Orange and lemon groves, and parterres of flowers intervene to dispel the monotony of the buildings, while on every side the tamarind and the cocoa-nut palm spread their welcome shade.

Jaggat Singh was a highly respected prince, and did much to efface the remembrance of the rude visitations of the Moguls. The dignity of his character, his benevolence of address and personal demeanour, secured the homage of all who had access to him, and are alike attested by the pen of the emperor, the ambassador of England, and the chroniclers of Mewar. He had the proud satisfaction of redeeming the ancient capital from ruin, rebuilding the Chaplet bastion which had been blown up by Akbar, restoring the portals, and replacing the pinnacles on the temple of Chattarkot. By a princess of Mewár he left two sons, the elder of whom succeeded him.

This son, Ráj Singh, the "royal lion," mounted the throne in 1654. Various causes, over which he had no control, combined, together with his personal

Photo by] [*Donald Macbeth, London*

ISLAND AND PALACE OF JAGMANDAR.

[p. 120

character, to break the long repose his country had enjoyed. The emperor of the Moguls had reached extreme old age, and the ambition of his sons to usurp his authority involved every Rájpút in support of their individual pretensions. The Rána inclined to Dárá, the legitimate heir to the throne, as did nearly the whole Rájpút race. But the battle of Fatehábád gave the lead to Aurangzeb, and he maintained it by the sacrifice of every thing that opposed his ambition. His father, his brothers, nay, his own offspring, were in turn victims to that thirst for power which eventually destroyed the monarchy of the Moguls.

The policy introduced by their founder, from which Jahángír and Shah Jáhán had reaped so many advantages, was unwisely abandoned by Aurangzeb who had more powerful reasons than either of the former for maintaining those ties which bound the Rájpút princes to his throne. His Tartar blood brought no Rájpút sympathies to his aid; on the contrary, every family shed its best blood in withstanding his accession, and in the defence of the rights of Shah Jahán, so long as there was any hope of success. Aurangzeb was not blind to this defect, and he tried to remedy it in his successor, for both his declared heir, Shah Alam, as well as Azím, and his favourite grandson, were the offspring of Rájpútnis. But, uninfluenced himself by such predilections, he allowed his bigotry to outweigh his policy, and he visited the Rájpúts with unrelenting persecution.

It has seldom occurred that so many distinguished princes were contemporary with one another as during the reign of Aurangzeb. Every Rájpút principality had a head above mediocrity in courage and ability. Jai Singh of Ambar, Jaswant Singh of Márwár, the Haras of Búndi and Kotah, the Rahtors of Bíkanír, Orcha, and Dattia, were all men who, had their prejudices been properly consulted, would have rendered the Mogul power indissoluble. But the emperor had but one measure of contumely for all, which not only withdrew every sentiment of support from the princes of Rájasthán, but stirred the heart of Siváji to strike for the freedom of Maháráshtra. In subtlety and the most specious hypocrisy, in that concentration of resolve which confides its deep purpose to none, in every qualification of the warrior and, we may add, the scholar, Aurangzeb had no equal amongst the many distinguished men of his race; but that sin by which fell the angels, steeped him in an ocean of guilt, and not only neutralised his natural capacities, but converted the means for unlimited power into an engine of destruction. "This hypocrisy," says the eloquent Orme, "increased with his power, and in order to palliate to his Muhammadan subjects the crimes by which he had become their sovereign, he determined to enforce the conversion of the Hindus by the severest penalties, and even by the sword; as if the blood of his subjects were to wash away the stains from his hands, already encrimsoned with that of his family. Labour left the field and industry the loom, until the decrease of the revenues induced Aurangzeb to substitute a capitation tax as the balance of account between the two religions." The same historian justly characterises this enactment as one so contrary to all notions of sound policy, as well as of the feelings of humanity, that "reflection seeks the motive with amazement." In this amazement we might remain, nor seek to develop the motive, did not the ample page of history in all nations disclose that, in the name of religion, more blood has been shed, and more atrocity committed, than by the united action of the whole catalogue of the passions.

Raj Singh had signalised his accession by the revival of warlike *tika-dour*, and plundered Malpúra, which, though on the Ajmír frontier, Shah Jahan refrained from avenging, replying to those who advised him to such a course, that "it was only a folly of his nephew." Later on, the impetuous prince threw down the gauntlet to Aurangzeb in the plenitude of his power, and the valour of the Sesodias again burst forth in all the splendour of the days of Partáp, the contest closing with a series of brilliant victories, and the narrow escape from captivity of the Xerxes of Hindustan. The Mogul demanded the hand of the princess of Rúpnagar, a junior branch of the Márwár house, and sent with the demand, compliance with which was regarded as certain, a *cortège* of 2000 horse to escort the fair to court. But the haughty Rájpútni rejected with disdain the proffered alliance, and entrusted her cause to the arm of the chief of the Rájpút race, offering herself as the reward for protection. The family priest, her preceptor, deemed his office honoured by being chosen the messenger of her wishes, and the letter he carried is incorporated in the annals of Mewár. "Is the swan to be the mate of the stork? A Rájpútni, pure in blood to be wife to the monkey-faced barbarian?" So wrote the princess, concluding with a threat of self-destruction if not saved from dishonour.

This appeal was seized on with avidity by the

Rana as a pretext for throwing away the scabbard, and embarking on a warfare in which he determined to put all to the hazard in defence of his country and his faith. The first step was an omen of success to his warlike and superstitious vassalage. With a chosen band he rapidly passed the foot of the Arávalli and appeared before Rúpnagar, cut up the imperial guards, and bore off the prize to his capital. This daring act was applauded by all who bore the name of Rájpút, and his chiefs with joy gathered their retainers round the red standard to protect the queen so gallantly rescued.

For a space the Mogul delayed his vengeance; and it was not until the deaths of Jaswant Singh of Márwár and Jai Singh of Ambar, both poisoned by his own command, that he deemed himself strong enough to put forth the full extent of his long-cherished design, the imposition of the *jezia*, or capitation tax, on the whole Hindu race. But he miscalculated his measures; and the murder of these two princes, far from advancing his aim, recoiled with vengeance on his head. The mother of Ajít, the infant heir of Márwár, a woman of the most determined character, was a princess of Mewár; and she threw herself upon the protection of the Rána as the natural guardian of her child during the dangers of his minority. The child was sent to reside at Kailwa under the safeguard of the brave Dúrga Dás, while the mother returned to Márwár to foster the spirit of resistance amongst the Rahtor clans. A unity of interests was thus cemented between these two powerful states such as had never existed between them before; and, but for the repeated instances of humanity on the part of the Rána, the throne of the Moguls might have been completely overturned.

On the promulgation of the *jezia*, the Rána remonstrated by letter with the emperor—a letter which for the grace and dignity of its style, and the lofty yet temperate resolution which characterises its tone, deserves to be quoted in full. The following is the translation of Sir W. B. Rouse:—

Letter from Rána Ráj Sing to Arungzeb.

All due praise be rendered to the glory of the Almighty, and the munificence of your majesty, which is conspicuous as the sun and moon. Although I, your well-wisher, have separated myself from your sublime presence, I am nevertheless zealous in the performance of every bounden act of obedience and loyalty. My ardent wishes and strenuous services are employed to promote the prosperity of the Kings, Nobles, Mirzas, Rajahs, and Roys, of the provinces of Hindostan, and the chiefs of Æraun, Turaun, Room, and Shawn, the inhabitants of the seven climates, and all persons travelling by land and by water. This my inclination is notorious, nor can your royal wisdom entertain a doubt thereof. Reflecting therefore on my former services, and your majesty's condescension, I presume to solicit the royal attention to some circumstances, in which the public as well as private welfare is greatly interested.

I have been informed, that enormous sums have been dissipated in the prosecution of the designs formed against me, your well-wisher; and that you have ordered a tribute to be levied to satisfy the exigencies of your exhausted treasury.

May it please your majesty, your royal ancestor Mahomed Jelaul ul Deen Akbar, whose throne is now in heaven, conducted the affairs of this empire in equity and firm security for the space of fifty-two years, preserving every tribe of men in ease and happiness, whether they were followers of Jesus, or of Moses, of David, or Mahomed; were they Brahmins, were they of the sect of Dharians, which denies the eternity of matter, or of that which ascribes the existence of the world to chance, they all equally enjoyed his countenance and favour: in so much that his people, in gratitude for the indiscriminate protection he afforded them, distinguished him by the appellation of *Juggut Gooroo* (Guardian of Mankind).

His majesty Mahomed Noor ul Deen Jehangheer, likewise, whose dwelling is now in paradise, extended, for a period of twenty-two years, the shadow of his protection over the heads of his people; successful by a constant fidelity to his allies, and a vigorous exertion of his arm in business.

Nor less did the illustrious Shah Jehan, by a propitious reign of thirty-two years, acquire to himself immortal reputation, the glorious reward of clemency and virtue.

Such were the benevolent inclinations of your ancestors. Whilst they pursued these great and generous principles, wheresoever they directed their steps, conquest and prosperity went before them; and then they reduced many countries and fortresses to their obedience. During your majesty's reign, many have been alienated from the empire, and farther loss of territory must necessarily follow, since devastation and rapine now universally prevail without restraint. Your subjects are trampled under foot, and every province of your empire is impoverished; depopulation spreads, and difficulties accumulate. When indigence has reached the habitation of the sovereign and his princes, what can be the condition of the nobles? As to the soldiery, they are in murmurs; the merchants complaining, the Mahomedans discontented, the Hindoos destitute, and multitudes of people, wretched even to the want of their nightly meal, are beating their heads throughout the day in rage and desperation.

How can the dignity of the sovereign be preserved, who employs his power in exacting heavy tributes from a people thus miserably reduced? At this juncture it is told from east to west, that the emperor of Hindostan, jealous of the poor Hindoo devotee, will exact a tribute from Brahmins, Sanorahs, Joghies, Berawghies, Sanyasees; that, regardless of the illustrious honour of his Timurean race, he condescends to exercise his power over the solitary inoffensive anchoret. If your majesty places any faith in those books, by distinction called divine, you will there be instructed, that God is the God of all mankind, not the God of Mahomedans alone.

The Pagan and the Mussulman are equally in His presence. Distinctions of colour are of His ordination. It is He who gives existence. In your temples, to His name the voice is raised in prayer; in a house of images, where the bell is shaken, still He is the object of adoration. To vilify the religion or customs of other men, is to set at naught the pleasure of the Almighty. When we deface a picture, we naturally incur the resentment of the painter; and justly has the poet said, presume not to arraign or scrutinize the various works of power divine.

In fine, the tribute you demand from the Hindoos is repugnant to justice : it is equally foreign from good policy, as it must impoverish the country : moreover, it is an innovation and an infringement of the laws of Hindostan. But if zeal for your own religion hath induced you to determine upon this measure, the demand ought, by the rules of equity, to have been made first upon Ramsing, who is esteemed the principal amongst the Hindoos. Then let your well-wisher be called upon, with whom you will have less difficulty to encounter; but to torment ants and flies is unworthy of an heroic or generous mind. It is wonderful that the ministers of your government should have neglected to instruct your majesty in the rules of rectitude and honour.

xi.—The Struggle with Aurangzeb

THIS letter, the sanctuary afforded to Ajít, and the carrying off of the lady of his choice, roused Aurangzeb to the highest pitch of resentment, and his hostile preparations more resembled those for the subjugation of a powerful kingdom than of a vassal chieftain whose domain was but a speck on the surface of his own colossal empire. The very magnitude of these preparations was the highest compliment to the tributary Rájpút; for the Suzerain of Hindustan denuded the very extremities of his empire before he had collected a force which he judged sufficient for his undertaking. Akbar was recalled from his province, Bengal, Azím from the distant Cábul, and Shah Alam, his heir, from the war in the Dekhan.

Having collected his formidable array, the emperor entered Mewár. He speedily reduced the low countries, for the Rájpúts had learnt by experience that this portion of their territory was indefensible against overwhelming odds, and the inhabitants had already retired with their effects to the hills. Chítor and many other strongholds were seized and garrisoned by the Moguls. Meanwhile, the Rána was animating the might of the Arávalli, where he meditated a resistance proportionate to the peril which threatened him — not the mere defence of dominion, but a struggle, *pro aris et focis*, around which rallied every Rájpút with the

Photo by] [*Donald Macbeth, London*

VIEW IN THE VALLEY OF UDAIPUR.

most deadly determination. Even the primitive races of the western wilds, "with thousands of bows and hearts devoted to the cause of Hindupat," assembled around the crimson banner.

The Rána divided his forces into three bodies. His eldest son, Jai Singh, was posted on the crest of the Arávalli, ready to act on the invaders from either side of the mountains; Prince Bhím was to the west, to keep up communications with Gujarát; while the Rána, with the main body, took post in the Nain defile, unassailable by the enemy, but hanging on his left flank, and ready to turn it as soon as the mountains were entered. The Girwoh, *i.e.* "circle," as the valley of the capital is named, is in form an irregular elipse, of about fourteen miles in length from north to south, and eleven in breadth, the capital being situated towards the extremity of the transverse axis, having only the Peshola lake between it and the base of the Arávalli. The hills bordering the valley range in height from eight hundred to twelve hundred feet, their fantastic peaks rising one above the other in every diversity of form. Towards the plains eastwards, it has three practicable passes, one in the north at Dailwára, a second more central near Dobári, and a third, that of Nain, leading to the intricacies of Chappan in the south. Of these passes the emperor chose the middle one as being the most practicable, and encamped near the Udai Ságar lake, on the left of its entrance. He then advanced to Dobári at the very mouth of the gorge; but, instead of entering it, he halted his force, and, by the advice of Tibúr Khán, sent on Prince Akbar with 50,000 men to the capital. This caution of the wily monarch saved him from the ably planned scheme of the Rájpút; otherwise, not only his son's force, but his entire army would have been trapped.

Prince Akbar advanced. Not a soul interrupted his progress to the city. Palaces, gardens, lakes, and isles, met his eye, but no living thing; all was silence. Accustomed to entering towns deserted through fear of his licentious soldiery, Akbar felt no apprehensions. His camp was pitched, his men were already enjoying the unwonted rest and security, when suddenly, as if from the clouds, the heir of Mewár with his whole force was upon them. "Some were praying, some feasting, some at chess; they came to steal, and yet fell asleep." In a few moments they were dispersed with terrific and unrelenting slaughter. Cut off from the possibility of a junction with the emperor by a movement of a part of the Rána's force, Akbar attempted a retreat to the plains of Márwár by the route of Gogúnda. It was a choice of evils, and he took the worst. The Bhíls of the mountains outstripped his retreat, and blocked up further egress in one of those long valleys closed by a natural rampart, or *col*, on which they formed *abbatics* of trees, and, manning the crests on either side, hurled destruction on the foe; while the prince, with equal speed, blocked up the entrance. Death menaced the Moguls on every side; at the hands of their enemies if they tried to escape, by starvation if they remained where they were. It was only the humanity of the Rána that saved them from annihilation. He admitted overtures, confided in protestations to renounce the object of the war, and sent guides to conduct them through the defile of Jilwára, nor did they halt till protected by the walls of Chitor.

Almost at the same time another body of the Imperialists, under the celebrated Delhír Khán, who attempted to enter from Márwár by the Daisúri pass (probably with a view to extricating Akbar), was assailed in the long intricate gorge by the chiefs of Rúpnagar and Ganora, and after a desperate conflict was entirely destroyed. On each occasion, a vast booty fell into the hands of the Rájpúts.

The Rána next gave the signal for a general attack on Aurangzeb, who was still at Dobári, watching with his son the result of the operations under Akbar and Delhír. The great home-clans had more than their wonted rivalry to sustain them, for Dúrga Dás and his Rahtor warriors were to combat with them against the common oppressor; and nobly did they contest the palm of glory. Aurangzeb could not withstand the onset. His guns, though manned by Franks, were unable to protect him against the just cause and avenging steel of the Rájpúts, and he was beaten and compelled to disgraceful flight, with an immense loss in men and equipment. The Rána had to lament many brave leaders, home and auxiliary; but the imperial standard, elephants, and state equipage, fell into his hands. This glorious encounter occurred in the spring of 1681.

The discomfited forces formed a junction under the walls of Chítor, whence the emperor dictated the recall of his son, Prince Alam, from the Dekhan, deeming it of greater moment to regain lost importance in the north, than to prevent the independence of Siváji. Meanwhile, the activity of Sawal Dás, a descendant of the famous Jaimal, cut off his communications between Chítor and Ajmír, and alarmed the tyrant for his personal safety. Leaving, therefore, this perilous warfare to his sons Azím and Akbar, with instructions how to act till reinforced, he quitted Mewár, and, at the head of his guards, repaired to Ajmír. Thence he despatched Khán Rohilla, with 12,000 men against Sawal Dás, with supplies and equipments for his sons. The Rahtor, joined by all the troops of Márwár, met and gave him battle at Púr Mandal. The Imperialists were defeated with great loss, and driven back on Ajmír.

While the Rána, his heirs and auxiliaries, were thus triumphant in all their operations, Prince Bhím with the left division was not idle, but made a powerful diversion by the invasion of Gujarát, captured Idar, expelling Hassan and his garrison, and proceeding by Birnagar, suddenly appeared before Patan, the residence of the provincial satrap, which place he plundered. Sidpúr and other towns shared the same fate, and he was in full march for Súrat when the benevolence of the Rána, touched by the woes of the fugitives who came to demand his forbearance, caused him to recall Bhím in the midst of his career.

Díal Sah, the civil minister of Mewár, and a man of high courage and activity, headed another flying force, which ravaged Málwa to the Narbadda and the Betwa. Sarangpúr, Mandu, Ujjain, and Chandéri were plundered, and numerous garrisons put to the sword. For once the Rájpúts avenged themselves, in imitation of the tyrant, on the religion of their adversaries: the *kázis* were bound and shaved, and the Koráns thrown into wells. The minister was unrelenting, and made Málwa a desert, and from the fruits of his incursions repaired the resources of his master. Flushed with success, he formed a junction with the heir of Mewár, and gave battle to Azím at Chítor. On this occasion, the flower of Mewár with the Rahtor and Khíchí auxiliaries was engaged, and obtained a glorious victory, the Mogul prince being defeated and pursued with great slaughter to Rinthambúr, which he entered. This was a just revenge, for it was Azím who had surprised Chítor in the preceding year.

In Mewár the contest terminated with the expulsion of the Imperialists from the country. The Rána, thereupon, in support of the minor prince of Márwár, united his arms to the forces of that state, and opened a new campaign at Ganora, the chief town of Godwár. The heroic mother of the infant prince had, since the death of her husband, resisted every aggression, and had on more than one occasion inflicted loss on her antagonists. Prince Bhím commanded the Sesodias. He formed a junction with the Rahtors, and the combined force gave battle to the royal troops led by Akbar and Tibúr Khán, and won a complete victory. Their success is attributed to the stratagem of a Rájpút chief, who, having captured 500 camels from the Imperialists, conceived the idea of fixing lighted torches to their heads and driving them into the royal camp; and in the confusion which resulted the Rájpúts carried out their attack.

On their continued success, the Rána and his allies meditated the project of dethroning the tyrant, and setting up his son Akbar in his place. Akbar received the proposal with favour, but he lacked the circumspection which characterised Aurangzeb, whose penetration defeated the scheme when on the eve of execution. The Rájpút army had already united with Akbar, and the astrologer had fixed the day which was to exalt him; but the revealer of secrets baffled his own prediction by disclosing it to the emperor. Aurangzeb, attended only by his guards at Ajmír, had recourse to the same stratagem which had raised him to the throne. There was no time to be lost, for Akbar was close at hand, and it would be long before Shah Alam and Azím could come to his assistance. He penned a letter to his son which was dropped by a spy in the tent of the Rájpút leader, Dúrga Dás. The letter applauded a pretended scheme by which Akbar was to fall upon the Rájpúts when they engaged the emperor. The ruse succeeded. The Rájpúts detached themselves from the prince, who had apparently betrayed them. Tibúr Khán, in despair, lost his life in an attempt to assassinate the emperor, and before the artifice was discovered, the reinforcements under Shah Alam and Azím arrived, and Aurangzeb was saved. The Rájpúts still offered refuge to Akbar; but, aware of his father's vigour of character, he deemed himself unsafe in his neighbourhood. He accepted, however, an escort of 5,000 horse, led by Dúrga Dás, and was conducted, in spite of every opposition, through the defiles of Mewár to the Mahrátta leader, Sambáji, at Palárgarh, whence he was shortly afterwards conveyed in an English ship to Persia.

"The escape of Akbar," observes Orme, "to Sambáji oppressed Aurungzebe with as much anxiety, as formerly the phantom of his brother Sujah amongst the Pathans; and the consequence of their alliance became a nearer care than the continuance of the war against the Rajpoots, whose gallant activity

Photo by] DÚRGU DÁS [*Donald Macbeth, London*

[*p.* 134

prevented a speedy decision by the sword; but the dignity of the throne precluded any overtures of peace to a resistance which had attempted the deposal, if not the life, of the monarch. A Rajpoot officer, who had long served with distinction under Delhir Khán, solved the difficulty: he quitted the army under pretence of retiring to his own country and visited the Rana, as from courtesy, on his journey. The conversation turned on the war, which the Rajpoot perhaps really lamented, and he persuaded the Rana that though Aurungzebe would never condescend to make, he might accept overtures of peace: upon which he was empowered by the Rana to tender them." "The domestic annals confirm this account, and give the name of this mediator, Rája Shiam Singh of Bikanir; but the negotiation was infamously protracted to the rains, the period when operations necessarily cease, and by which time Aurangzeb had recruited his broken forces; and it was concluded "without assertion or release of the capitation tax, but with the surrender of the districts taken from Chitor, and the state of Jodhpur was included in the treaty."

Once more, we claim the reader's admiration on behalf of a patriot prince of Mewár, and ask him to contrast the indigenous Rájpút with the emperor of the Moguls. Aurangzeb accumulated on his head more crimes than any prince who ever sat on an Asiatic throne. With all the disregard of life which marks his nation, he was never betrayed, even in the fever of success, into a single generous action; and, contrary to the prevailing principle of our natures, the moment of his foe's submission was that chosen for the completion of his malignant revenge. How opposite to the benevolence of the Rájpút prince who, when the most effectual means of self-defence lay in the destruction of the resources of his enemy, out of pity for a suffering population, recalled his son in the midst of victory! As a skilful general and gallant soldier, Ráj Singh is above praise. The manner in which, in spite of all consequences, he espoused the cause of the Márwár princess, places him in the highest rank of chivalry; while his dignified letter of remonstrance to Aurangzeb on the promulgation of the *jezia* affords a striking proof of his moral and intellectual greatness. His taste for the arts is evidenced by the formation of the inland lake, the Rájsamand, with a brief account of which, and the motives for its construction, we shall conclude the sketch of this glorious epoch in the annals of Mewár.

This great national work is twenty-five miles north of the capital, and is situated on a declivity of the plain about two miles from the base of the Arávalli. A small perennial stream, called the Gumti, flowing from these mountains, was arrested in its course, and confined by an immense embankment made to form the lake, called after himself, Rájsamand, or the "royal sea." The *band*, or dam, forms an irregular segment of a circle, embracing an extent of nearly three miles. It confines a sheet of water of great depth, and about twelve miles in circumference. It is entirely of white marble, with a flight of steps of the same material throughout its extent from the summit to the water's edge; and the whole is buttressed by an enormous mound of earth, on which trees were planted, and a promenade formed. On the south side are the town and fortress built by the Rána, and called after him, Rájnaggar; and upon the embankment stands the temple of Kankarauli, the shrine of one of the seven forms of Krishna, ornamented with sculpture and inlaid work, the design on one of the walls being a genealogical tree of the founder's family. One million one hundred and fifty thousand pounds sterling, contributed by the Rána, his chiefs, and the more opulent of his subjects, was expended on these works, of which the material was from the adjacent quarries. But magnificent, costly, and useful as is the Rájsamand, it derives its chief beauty from the benevolent motive to which it owes its birth—namely, the alleviation of the miseries of a starving population during one of those awful visitations of famine and pestilence with which these states are from time to time afflicted.

It was in 1661, seven years after the accession of Ráj Singh, that these combined evils reached Mewár, less subject to them, owing to its natural advantages, than any other state in India; and the chief, deeply meditating on the extreme distress of his subjects, determined to raise a monument by which the wretched might be supported, and his own name perpetuated. The lake occupied seven years in construction, and at its commencement and termination, all the rites of sacrifice and oblation were observed. The Rána went to implore favour at the temple of the "four-armed," for though the season of the monsoon was passed, not a drop of rain had fallen; and in like manner the next two months passed away. "For want of water the world was in despair, and people went mad with hunger. Things unknown as food were eaten. The husband abandoned the wife, parents sold their children, while time served only to increase the evil. Even the insects and fishes died, for they had nothing to feed upon. Thousands of all ages became victims to hunger. Those who procured food to-day, ate twice what they required. The wind was from the west, a pestilential vapour. The constellations were always visible at night, nor was there a cloud in the sky by day, and thunder and lightning were unknown. Such portents filled mankind with dread. The ministers of religion forgot their duties. There was no longer distinction of caste, and the Sudra and Brahmin were undistinguishable. Fruits, flowers, and every vegetable thing, were devoured, and even trees were striped of their bark to appease the cravings of hunger. Cities were depopulated, the seed of whole families lost, and the hopes of all extinguished."[1]

Such is the simple yet terrific record of this pestilence from which Mewár was hardly freed when Aurangzeb commenced the religious war just narrated, which, with all its atrocities, still further devastated this fair region.

[1] From the *Ráj Vilas*, the Chronicles of the reign of Ráj Singh.

xii.—The Struggle Continued

RÁNA JAI SINGH took possession of the *gadi* in 1681. A circumstance occurred at his birth which is worthy of narration, as illustrating the importance in the eyes of the Rájpút of his national customs and rites. A few hours after the appearance of Jai Singh, the Rána's other, and favourite, wife also gave birth to a son called Bhím. It is customary for the father to bind round the arm of a new-born infant a root of that species of grass called *amirdhob*, the "imperishable," and well known for its nutritive properties and luxuriant vegetation under the most intense heat. The Rána first attached the ligature round the arm of the younger, apparently by an oversight, though, in fact, from superior affection for his mother. As the boys approached to manhood, the Rána, apprehensive that this preference might create dissension, one day drew his sword, and, placing it in the hand of Bhím, the elder, said, it was better to use it at once on his brother, than thereafter to endanger the safety of the state. This appeal to his generosity had an instantaneous effect, and he not only took an oath "by his father's throne" never to dispute the sovereign rights of his brother, but declared, to remove all fears, "he was not his son if he again drank water within the pass of Dobári"; and, collecting his retainers, he abandoned Udaipúr to court fortune where she might be kinder. He proceeded to the court of Bahádur Shah, who conferred upon him the dignity of a leader of 3,500 horse, with the revenues of 52 districts for their support; but quarrelling with the imperial general, he was despatched with his contingent west of the Indus, where he died.

Jai Singh concluded a treaty with Aurangzeb, conducted within the boundaries of Mewár by the princes Azím and Delhír Khán, who took every occasion to testify their gratitude for the clemency the royal forces had met with in the recent campaign. On this occasion, the Rána was attended by 10,000 horse and 40,000 foot, besides the multitudes collected from the mountains to view the ceremony, above 100,000 souls, who set up a shout of joy at the prospect of once more returning in safety to their homes in the plains. That the treaty was advantageous to the Rána we may infer from the fact that the sons of Delhír were left behind as hostages for the good faith of the Mogul. On bidding the Rána farewell, Delhír remarked: "Your nobles are rude, and my children are hostages for your safety; but if at the expense of their lives I can regain possession of your country, you may keep your mind at ease, for there was friendship between my father and yours."

But all other protection than what his sword afforded was futile; and though Delhír's intentions were noble, he had little control over events. In less than five years after his accession, the Rána was again forced "to fly the plains" for the inaccessible haunts of his native fastnesses. Yet, in spite of these untoward circumstances and uninterrupted warfare, such were the resources of his little state that he was able to undertake and complete a work which still perpetuates his name. He drew a dam across a break in the mountains, the channel of an ever-flowing stream, by which he formed one of the largest lakes in India, giving it his own name, the Jaisamand, or "sea of victory." Nature had furnished the hint for this undertaking, for there had always existed a considerable volume of water; but the Rána had the merit of uniting the natural buttresses and converting the Dhíbur Pul into a little inland sea. The circumference cannot be less than 30 miles, and the benefits to cultivation, and especially to the growing of rice, which requires constant irrigation, were great. On this huge rampart he erected a palace for his favourite queen, Comála Devi, familiarly known as the Rúta Ráni, or "testy queen."

Domestic unhappiness appears to have generated in the Rána inaptitude for state affairs; and, unluckily, the favoured queen estranged him from his son. The latter was called Amra, a name highly venerated in Mewár. His mother was of the Búndi house, whose representatives had, in times past, performed great services for, and brought great calamities upon, the Sesodia princes. To the jealousies of the rival queens, one of them mother to the heir, and the other the favourite of the sovereign, are attributed dissensions which at such a juncture were a greater misfortune than the loss of a battle, and which afford another illustration, if any were wanting, of the impolicy of polygamy.

Rána Jai Singh, who had evinced such gallantry in the wars of Aurangzeb, secluded himself with Comála in the retreat, Jaisamand, leaving Amra, under the guidance of the minister, at the capital.

But the latter, having personally insulted this chief officer of the state, in consequence of receiving a rebuke for turning loose an infuriated elephant in the city, the Rána left his retreat and came to Udaipúr. Amra did not await his father's arrival, but fled to Búndi and took up arms, and, joined by many of his own nobles and Hara auxiliaries, returned at the head of 10,000 men. The Rána, desirous of averting civil war, retired to Godwár beyond the Arávalli, whence he sent the Ganora chief to expostulate with his son. Amra made for Komulmír, with a view to securing the state treasure; but, failing in this attempt, and seeing the determination of the chiefs who were faithful to the Rána, he made terms with the ambassador. The compact was ratified at the shrine of Eklinga, and, in obedience to its conditions, Amra remained an exile from Mewár until the conclusion of his father's life. Jai Singh died twenty years after his accession. Had he maintained the reputation of his early years, he might have redeemed his country's independence, for the times were well suited to such an endeavour. But documents yet exist which prove that, in his later life, a state of indolence, having all the effects of imbecility, supervened, and, but for the formation of the Jaisamand lake, his reign would have remained a blank in the annals of the state.

Amra II. who succeeded in 1700 had much of the gallantry and active turn of mind of his illustrious namesake; but the degrading conflict with his father had much impaired the moral strength of the country, and counteracted the advantages which might have resulted from the decline of the Mogul power. The reigns of Ráj Singh and Jai Singh illustrate the obvious truth, that on the personal character of the chief of a feudal government everything depends. The former, infusing by his talents and energy patriotic sentiments into all his subordinates, vanquished in a series of conflicts the vast military resources of the empire, led by the emperor, his sons, and chosen generals; while his successor, heir to this moral strength, and with every collateral aid, lowered her to a stage of contempt from which no talent could subsequently raise her.

Amra early availed himself of the contentions amongst the sons of Aurangzeb, and formed a secret treaty with the Mogul heir-apparent, Shah Alam, whilst that prince was commanding in the countries west of the Indus. The events of this period are of special importance, for they not only involved the overthrow of the Mogul empire, but originated that state of society which paved the way for the dominion of Great Britain. When Aurangzeb despised and trampled upon the traditions and sentiments of the Rájpúts, he endangered the key-stone of his power, and before his death the enormous fabric reared by Akbar was tottering to its very foundations; demonstrating to conviction, that the highest order of talent, whether for government or war, though aided by unlimited resources, will not suffice for the maintenance of power, unsupported by the affections of the governed. When Aurangzeb became emperor, he could, had he chosen to do so, have gained the whole-hearted support of his Hindu subjects. But the most devoted attachment and the most faithful service were repaid by insult to their habits, and the imposition of an obnoxious tax; and to the *jezia*, and the unwise pertinacity with which his successors enforced it, must be directly ascribed the overthrow of the monarchy. No condition was exempted from this odious and impolitic assessment, which was deemed by the tyrant a mild substitute for the conversion he once meditated of the entire Hindu race to the creed of Islam.

An abandonment of faith was the surest road to the tyrant's favour, and it was an example of this dereliction which powerfully contributed to the annihilation of the empire. Rao Gopál, a kinsman of the Rána, held the fief of Rampúra, on the Chambal, and was serving with a select quota of his clan in the wars of the Dekhan, when his son, who had been left at home, withheld the revenues, which he applied to his own use instead of remitting them to his father. Rao Gopál complained to the emperor; but the son discovered that he could, by a sacrifice, not only appease Aurangzeb, but attain the object of his wishes. He apostatised from his faith, and won the emperor's forgiveness, and with it the domain of Rampúra. Rao Gopál fled the royal camp in disgust, made an unsuccessful attempt to regain his estate, and then took refuge with Rána Amra. The asylum granted to a chief of his own kin was construed by the emperor into a signal for revolt, and Azím was ordered to Málwa to watch the Rána's movements. The Rána took up arms, and Málwa joined the tumult, while, at the same time, there took place the first irruption of the Mahráttas across the Narbadda. Amidst these accumulated troubles, his Rájpút feudatories disgusted and alienated, his sons and grandsons already quarrelling over the succession, and the Mahráttas rising into dangerous prominence, did Aurangzeb, after a reign of terror of half a century's duration, breathe his last. He had reached the age of ninety years, and his death took place at the city bearing his name, Aurangábád, in 1707.

At his death, his second son Azím assumed the imperial dignity, and, aided by the Rájpút princes of Dattia and Kotah, who had always served in his division, marched to Agra to contest the legitimate claims of his brother Shah Alam who was advancing from Cábul, supported by the contingents of Mewár and Márwár, and all western Rájasthán. The battle of Jajao which followed was fatal to Azím, who, with his son Bédarbakt, and the princes of Dattia and Kotah, was slain, and his brother ascended the throne under the title of Shah Alam Bahádur Shah. This prince had many qualities which might have endeared him to the Rájpúts. Had he immediately succeeded the beneficent Shah Jahán, the race of Timúr, in all human probability, would still have been enthroned at Delhi. But Aurangzeb had inflicted an incurable wound on the Hindu race, which for ever estranged them from his successors; nor were the virtues of Bahádur, during the short lustre of his sway, capable of healing it.

Bahádur Shah was soon made to perceive the little support he had in future to expect from the Rájpúts. Whilst he was engaged in quashing the pretensions of his youngest brother, Kambaksh, who had proclaimed himself emperor in the Dekhan, and in subduing a rising of the Sikhs in the north, a triple league was formed against him by the Rána of Mewár, Ajít Singh of Márwár, and the prince of Ambar. This treaty of unity of interests against the common foe was confirmed by nuptial alliances, such as had not taken place since the days of Partáp. In fact, to be readmitted to this honour with the Sesodias was one of the main considerations which led the princes of Márwár and Ambar to join the league. The parties renounced on oath all connection, domestic or political, with the imperial court. It was also stipulated that the sons of marriages sanctioned under the new treaty should be regarded as heirs, and that daughters should never be dishonoured by being betrothed to Moguls. As will be seen later, this stipulation originated many difficulties, for it compromised the right of primogeniture; and the umpire who was called upon to settle the disputes which ensued therefrom, proved more baneful than the power from whose iron grasp they were endeavouring to free themselves. The treaty laid prostrate the throne of Bábar, but it ultimately introduced the Mahráttas as partisans in their family disputes, who, in all such cases, made the bone of contention their own.

The injudicious support afforded by the emperor to the apostate chief of Rampúra first brought the triple federation into action. The Rána, upholding the cause of Gopál Rao, made an attack on Rampúra, which the usurper, now Rája Muslim Khán, succeeded in repelling, and was rewarded by the emperor. At the same time, information was conveyed to the Mogul court that "the Rána had determined to lay waste his territory, and retire to the hills"—a report which was speedily confirmed by the unwelcome news that Firoz Khán, the governor of Púr Mandal, had been attacked by the Rána's troops, and driven back, with great loss, to Ajmír. But ere Bahádur Shah could take measures to check these disorders, his career was cut short by poison. Had his life been spared, his talents, experience, and courteous manners might have retarded the downfall of his empire, which the utter unworthiness of his successor sunk beyond the power of man to redeem. Every subsequent succession was through blood. Two brothers, Syads from the town of Bareh in the Doáb, became all powerful at the Mogul court, setting up and plucking down its puppet kings at their pleasure. They had elevated Farrukhsiyar when the triumvirs of Rájasthán commenced their operations.

Giving loose to their long suppressed resentment, the Rájpúts abandoned altogether the spirit of toleration. They overthrew the mosques built on the sites of their altars, and treated the civil and religious officers of the government with indignity. Of these every town in Rájasthán had two, its *mullah* to proclaim the name of Muhammad, and its *kázi* for the administration of justice—a branch of administration entirely wrested from the hands of the native princes. The Syads made every effort to oppose the threatening measures of the Rájpúts, and at last succeeded in detaching Ajít Singh of Márwár from the league. Tempted by the offer of a powerful position at the Mogul court, he agreed to pay tribute, and gave a daughter in marriage to Farrukhsiyar.

This marriage considerably weakened the opposition of the Rájpúts, but it had another, and a more far-reaching result; for to it may, in a large measure, be ascribed the rise of British power in India. Farrukhsiyar was, at this time, suffering from a dangerous malady necessitating an operation which none of the royal physicians was able to perform; and the nuptial celebrations had, in consequence, to be postponed. A mission from the British merchants at Súrat was then at the court, and, as a last resource, the surgeon attached to it was called in. He cured the malady, and the emperor, made happy in his bride, displayed his gratitude with oriental magnificence. He desired Mr Hamilton to name his reward, and to the disinterested patriotism of this individual did the British owe the first royal grant, or firman, conferring territorial possession and great commercial privileges.

The weak Farrukhsiyar, desirous of snapping the leading-strings of the Syads, recalled to his court Ináyat Ulla Khán, the minister of Aurangzeb, and restored him to his office. Ináyat Ulla, to use the words of the historian of the period, "did not consult the temper of the times, so very different from the reign of Aurangzeb, and the revival of the *jezia* came with him." Though by no means severe in its operation, not amounting to three-quarters per cent. on annual income, from which the lame, the blind, and the very poor were exempt, it nevertheless raised a spirit of general hostility, particularly from its retaining the insulting distinction of a "tax on infidels." But if its incidence was less severe than formerly, the mode and channel of its introduction evinced to the Rájpút no hope that the intolerant spirit which originally suggested it would ever be subdued.

Rána Amra was not an idle spectator of these occurrences; and although the spurious thirst for distinction so early broke up the alliance by detaching Ajít from it, he redoubled his efforts for personal independence, and with it that of the Rájpút nation. An important document attests his solicitude, namely, a treaty with the emperor, which shows the altered relations which at this time existed between the parties. It consisted of the following eight clauses:—

Memorandum of Requests.

1st. The *mansab* of 7,000.
2nd. Firman of engagement under the *punja* private seal and sign that the *jezia* shall be abolished—that it shall no longer be imposed on the Hindu nation; at all events, that none of the Chagitai race shall authorise it in Mewár. Let it be annulled.
3rd. The contingent of one thousand horse for service in the Dekhan to be excused.
4th. All places of Hindu faith to be rebuilt, with perfect freedom of religious worship.
5th. If my uncles, brothers, or chiefs, repair to the presence, they are to meet no encouragement.
6th. The Bhomias of Deola, Banswára, Dongarpúr, and Sirohi, besides other zamindárs over whom I am to have control, shall not be admitted to the presence.
7th. The forces I possess are my chiefs—what troops you may require for a given period, you must furnish with rations (*paiti*), and when the service is over, their accounts will be settled.
8th. Of the Hakdárs, Zamindárs, Mansabdárs, who serve you with zeal and from the heart, let me have a list—and those who are not obedient I will punish; but in effecting this no demand is to be made for *paimali.*

The title of the treaty marks the subordination of the Rájpút; but while it is headed a "Memorandum of Requests," the eighth article discloses the effectual means of the Rána, for there he assumes an air of protection towards the emperor. In the stipulation for the *mansab* of 7,000, the mind reverts to the great Amra, who preferred to abdicate rather than acknowledge a superior; but opinion had undergone a great change since the days of Jahángír. In temporal dignities other states had risen to an equality with Mewár, and all had learnt to look on the Mogul as the dispenser of honours.

This treaty was the last act of Rána Amra's life. He died in 1716, leaving the reputation of an active and high-minded prince, who well upheld his station and the prosperity of his country, notwithstanding the anarchy of the period. His memory is held in high veneration; nor do the Rájpúts admit the absolute degradation of Mewár till the period of the second prince in succession to Amra.

xiii.—Break-up of the Mogul Empire

Amra was followed by Sangrám Singh, who reigned for eighteen years. He ascended the throne a year before the accession of Muhammad Shah, the last of the race of Timúr who deserved the name of emperor of India. During his reign, the empire of the Moguls was completely dismembered. In lieu of one paramount power, numerous independent governments started up, and preserved an uncertain existence until, in the course of a hundred years, they were brought, Muhammadan, Rájpút, and Mahrátta, under the dominion of the British. Like the satraps of the ancient Persian, or the lieutenants of Alexander, each chief proclaimed himself master of the province, the government of which had been confided to his loyalty and talents; and it cannot fail to diminish any regret at the successive prostration of Bengal, Oudh, and Hyderabad, and other less conspicuous states, to remember that they were founded in rebellion, and erected on ingratitude, and that their rulers were destitute of what alone could have given stability to their thrones, namely, sympathy with the condition of their subjects. With the Mahráttas the case is different. Their emergence to power claims our admiration, for it was the spirit of resistance to tyranny which transformed their husbandmen and ministers of religion into hardy and enterprising soldiers; and had their ambition been restrained within legitimate bounds, it would have been politically and morally just that the family of Siváji should retain its authority in countries which his valour had wrested from Aurangzeb. But the genius of conquest changed their natural habits. They devastated instead of consolidating; and in place of that severe and frugal simplicity and that energy of enterprise which were, in the beginning, their peculiar characteristics, they became distinguished for mean parsimony, low cunning, and dastardly depredation. Had they, retaining their original character, been content with their proper sphere of action, the Dekhan, they might yet have held the sovereignty of that vast region, where the habits and manners of the people were not incompatible with their own. But in the north the Mahrátta was a foreigner; and though professing the same creed as the Rájpút, he was, in sentiment, less akin to him than the Mogul, whose tyrannical intolerance was more endurable because less degrading than the rapacious meanness of the Southron.

The short reign of Farrukhsiyar was drawing to a close. The recall of Ináyat Ulla had proved but a feeble counterpoise to the thraldom of the Syads, while his arbitrary habits and the re-establishment of the *jezia* lost the unfortunate monarch all his Hindu supporters, including Ajít of Márwár, the father of his queen. It was at this time that the celebrated Nizám-ul-múlk, the founder of the Hyderabad state, was brought upon the stage. He was holding the unimportant charge of the district of Muradábád, and the Syads, knowing him to be a man of ability, bought him over to further their views by promising him the governorship of Málwa. Having thus strengthened their position, and with a body of 10,000 Mahráttas to support them, they suddenly declared the deposal of Farrukhsiyar, who was left without any assistance save that of the princes of Ambar and Búndi. Had he hearkened to their counsel to take the field and trust his cause to them, the situation might still have been saved. But, cowardly and infatuated, he refused to quit the walls of his palace, and threw himself upon the mercy of his enemies, who made him dismiss the faithful Rájpúts and admit a guard of honour of their troops into the citadel.

Farrukhsiyar hoped for security in the inviolability of the harem ; but even there he found no sanctuary. To use the words of the Mogul chronicle—"Night advanced, and the gates of the citadel were closed upon his friends. No one knew what was passing in the palace, and the troops under the Amír-ul-úmra, with 10,000 Mahráttas, remained under arms all the night. Morning came, and all hope was extinguished by the royal guard announcing the deposal of the emperor and the accession of his successor Rafi-ud-darját. The interval between the deposal and the death of an Asiatic king is short; and even while the heralds vociferated "long live the king" to the new puppet, the bow-string was on the neck of the contemptible Farrukhsiyar.

The first act of the new reign was one of conciliation towards Ajít Singh and the Rájpúts,—the abrogation of the *jezia* ; and the Syads still further showed their disposition to court their favour by dismissing Ináyat Ulla, and appointing to the high office of Díwán one of their own faith, Rája Rattan Chand. In the course of the next few months, three phantoms of royalty flitted across the scene, to be succeeded by Muhammad Shah, the eldest son of Bahádur Shah, during whose reign of nearly thirty years, the empire fell completely to pieces. The haughty demeanour of the Syads disgusted all who acted with them, especially their coadjutor the Nizám, whom, by reason of the talents he displayed in restoring Málwa to order, they regarded with suspicion and fear. It was impossible to cherish any abstract loyalty for the puppets they established, and the Nizám determined to make himself independent, and marched for the Dekhan. The brothers had good cause for alarm. The Rájpúts were recalled to their contingents, and the princes of Kotah and Nirwah gallantly interposed their own retainers to prevent the rebellious governor from crossing the Narbadda. But the attempt was futile; Kotah was slain, and the Nizám, taking possession of Barhanpúr, laid the foundations of the Hyderabad state.

The independence of Oudh was soon to follow. The founder of this kingdom was Sádat Khán, commandant of the garrison at Biána. He entered into a conspiracy with the emperor to overthrow the Syads. In the tumult which ensued, both the brothers were killed, and Sádat Khán was rewarded with the title of Bahádur Jang and the government of Oudh. The ties which bound him to the throne of Delhi were of the weakest, and before he died they were altogether severed. The Rájpúts took no part in these upheavals, and as a reward for their neutrality Muhammad Shah confirmed the repeal of the *jezia*, and appointed the Rája of Ambar to the government of Agra, and the Rája of Jodhpúr to that of Gujarát and Ajmír.

The policy of Mewár was too isolated for the times;

her rulers clung to forms and unsubstantial homage, while their neighbours, with more active vigour, plunged into the tortuous policy of the imperial court, and seized every opportunity to enlarge the boundaries of their states; and while Ambar appropriated to herself the royal domains almost to the Jumna, while Márwár planted her banner on the battlements of Ajmír, dismembered Gujarát, and pushed her clans far into the desert, Mewár confined her ambition to the control of her ancient feudatories of Abu, Idar, and the petty states which grew out of her, Dangarpúr and Banswára. The motive for this policy was precisely the same that had cost such sacrifices in former times; she dreaded amalgamating with the imperial court, and preferred political inferiority to the sacrifice of principle.

Rána Sangrám died in 1734. Under him Mewár was respected, and the greater portion of her lost territory was regained. Not a little of his success was due to the ability of his minister Behári Dás Pancholi, who was held in honourable regard by all the princes of Rájasthán. He held his office during three reigns; but his skill was unable to stem the tide of Mahrátta invasion, which commenced on the death of Sangrám.

Many anecdotes relating to Rána Sangrám have been preserved, some of which are worthy of perusal; for though the incidents recorded are trivial enough, they afford an insight into Rájpút life and ideas such as we can gain from no other source, and thereby aid us in our estimate of Rájpút character. These anecdotes uniformly represent the Rána as a patriarchal ruler, wise, just, and inflexible, steady in his application to business, and averse from all forms of extravagance, whether public or private. To regulate the latter, he made sumptuary laws which were rigidly adhered to, and on which the people still expatiate, contrasting with the existing profusion and luxury the simplicity and frugality of former days. On one occasion, it is related, the Chohan of Kotário, a chieftain of the first rank, recommended the Rána to make an addition to the folds of the court robe, and as courtesy forbade personal denial, his wish was assented to, and he retired to his estate pluming himself on his sovereign's acquiescence and his own influence. But, on his departure, the Rána sent for his minister, and commanded the sequestration of two villages of Kotário; which fact reaching the ears of the chieftain, he straightway repaired to court, and begged to know the fault which had drawn upon him this mark of displeasure. "None, Raoji," was the reply; "but on a minute calculation I find the revenue of these two villages will just cover the expense of the superfluity of garment which obedience to your wishes will occasion me; and as every iota of my own income is appropriated, I have no other means of complying with your suggestion than to make you bear the charge which it involves." It may readily be believed that the Chohan begged the revocation of the edict, and that he entertained for the future a higher regard for the sumptuary laws of the state.

On another occasion, from lapse of memory or want of consideration, the Rána himself broke one of the laws he had established, and alienated a village attached to the royal household. Each branch of the household expenditure had its appropriate fund, whether for the kitchen, the wardrobe, the privy purse, or the royal harem. Lands and villages set apart for this purpose were called *thua*, and each had its officer, or *thuadár*, who was accountable for his trust to the prime minister. The revenue from the particular village which the Rána had alienated was devoted to the provisioning of the royal kitchen; and when the Rána and his chiefs sat down in the *rassora*, or banqueting hall, to partake of the evening repast, there was no sugar forthcoming for the curds, a dish which has a place in the dinner *carte* of every Rájpút. The superintendent was called and upbraided for the omission. "*Anddáta*" (giver of food), replied the officer, "the minister says you have given away the village set apart for sugar."—"Just," said the Rána, and finished his meal without further remark, and without sugar to his curds.

A third anecdote illustrates the almost divine character with which the Ránas of Udaipúr were invested by their subjects. As Sangrám sat down to dinner one night, tidings arrived of an invasion of the Málwa Patháns, who had rifled several villages of Mandisor, carrying the inhabitants into captivity. Pushing his plate from him he ordered his armour, and the *nakara* to beat for the assemblage of his chieftains. With all speed, a gallant band formed on the terrace below; but they prevailed on the Rána to leave the punishment of the desultory aggression to them, as unworthy of his personal interference. Shortly after they had departed, the chief of Kanorh arrived, having left a sick bed to obey his sovereign's summons. In vain the prince endeavoured to keep him back, and he joined the band just as they came up with the invaders. The foe was defeated and put to flight, but the sick chieftain fell in the charge, and his son was severely wounded by his side. On the young chief repairing to court, he was honoured with the *bíra* from the chief's own hand, a distinction which he held to be an ample reward for his wounds and testimonial to the worth of his father. The *bíra* is the betel leaf folded up, containing aromatic spices, and presented to departing guests. The Kanorh chieftain being of the second grade of nobles, was not entitled to the distinction of receiving it from the sovereign's own hand.

Sangrám's reign was honourable to himself, and beneficial to his country, in whose defence he fought eighteen battles, and though his policy was too circumscribed, and his country would have been benefited by a surrender of some of those antique prejudices which kept her back in the general scramble for portions of the dilapidated kingdom of the Moguls, yet he was respected abroad and beloved by his own subjects. Rána Sangrám was the last prince who upheld the dignity of the throne of Bappa Ráwul; for, with the reign of his son and successor, commenced the period of Mahrátta ascendancy.

Jaggat Singh, the eldest of the four sons of Sangrám, succeeded in 1734. The commencement of his reign was signalised by a revival of the triple alliance formed by Rána Amra, and broken by Rája Ajít's connection with the Syads. The new engagement, which included all the minor states, was formed at Hurlah, a town in Mewár on the Ajmír frontier, where the confederate princes met at the head of their vassals. To insure unanimity, the Rána was invested with paramount control and the leadership of the forces. Had the Rájpúts adhered to their compact, they might have secured not only the independence but the aggrandisement of Rájasthán, and have defied alike the expiring efforts of Mogul tyranny and the Parthian-like warfare of the Mahráttas. They were, indeed, the most formidable power in India at this juncture. But even in the days when the Rána's superiority was unquestioned, it had never been an easy task to unite the princes of Rájasthán for mutual preservation; and now that Ambar and Márwár had attained positions equal to, if not higher than, that of Mewár, the difficulty was tenfold greater. The opportunities were many and splendid for the recovery of Rájpút freedom; but though individually enamoured of liberty, they would never submit to the control necessary for its realisation, and thus the best opportunity that had ever occurred was lost. A glance at the condition of the Mogul empire at the close of the Jaggat Singh's reign will make clear the comparative strength of the Rájpúts.

The Nizám had completely emancipated himself from his allegiance, and signalised his independence by sending to the emperor the head of the general who ventured to dispute it. He leagued with the Rájpúts, and instigated Báji Rao, the Mahrátta leader, to plant his standard in Málwa and Gujarát. Jai Singh of Ambar, who had been nominated governor of the former place, delegated it to the invader, and Málwa was lost. The extensive province of Gujarát shared the same fate, and was handed over by Ajít of Márwár, who, however, retained the most northern districts, which he added to his own territory. Shúja-ud-daula was supreme in Bengal, Behár, and Orissa, while Safdar Jang, the son of Sádat Khán, was established in Oudh. The basest disloyalty marked the rise of this last family, which owed everything to Muhammad Shah. It was Sádat Khán who brought about the sack of Delhi by Nádir Shah, which gave the last stab to the empire; and it was Safdar Jang who, when commander of the artillery, turned it against his sovereign's palace, and then conveyed it to Oudh. But we are anticipating.

The Mahrátta establishments in Málwa and Gujarát constituted a nucleus for others to form upon. They crossed the Narbadda in swarms, and many well-known names, such as the Holkárs, the Sindhias, and the Puárs, now began to emerge from obscurity. At this time they were united under one standard, that of Báji Rao. It was in 1735 that he first crossed the Chambal and appeared before Delhi, which he blockaded, and exacted *chouth*, or a fourth part of the revenues of the empire, as the price of his withdrawal. The Nizám, dreading the influence such pusillanimous concession might exert upon his rising power, determined to drive the Mahráttas out of Málwa, where, if once settled, they would cut off his communications with the north. He, accordingly, crossed the Narbadda, defeated Báji Rao in a pitched battle, and was only prevented from following up his victory by the advance of Nádir Shah from Afghanistan.

xiv.—Anarchy and Strife

In this new emergency, great hopes were placed on the valour of the Rájpúts; but the spirit of devotion in this brave race, by whose aid the Mogul power had been made and maintained, was irretrievably alienated, and not one of those high families who had been so lavish of their blood in defence of the imperial throne, obeyed the royal summons. A sense of common danger brought together some of the so-called feudatories, and the Nizám and Sádat Khán (now vizier of the empire) united their forces under the imperial commander. But their demoralised levies were no match for the Persian and the northern mountaineer. The Amír-ul-úmra was slain, the vizier made prisoner, and Muhammad Shah and his kingdom were at Nádir's disposal.

The disloyalty of the vizier filled the capital with blood, and reduced his sovereign to the condition of a captive. A ransom had already been arranged by the Nizám, who, in return for his diplomatic skill, had been raised to the office of Amír-ul-úmra, when Sádat Khán, stung by jealousy at his rival's promotion, stimulated the avarice of the conqueror by an exaggerated account of the riches of Delhi, and declared that he alone could furnish the amount negotiated by the Nizám. Nádir's love of gold overcame any scruples he may have had; the compact was broken; the keys of the city were demanded; and its humiliated emperor was led in triumph through the camp of his enemy, who, on the 8th March 1740, took possession of the palace of Timúr, and coined money bearing the legend,

> King over the kings of the world
> Is Nádir king of kings, and lord of the period.

The accumulated wealth of India, collected in the royal treasury, notwithstanding the lavish expenditure during the civil wars, and the profuse rewards scattered by each competitor for dominion, was yet sufficient to gratify even avarice itself, amounting in gold, jewels, and plate, to forty millions sterling, exclusive of equipages of every description. But this enormous spoil only kindled instead of satiating the appetite of Nádir, and a fine of two millions and a half was exacted, and levied with such unrelenting rigour and cruelty on the inhabitants, that men of rank and character could find no means of escape but by suicide. A rumour of this monster's death excited an insurrection, in which several Persians were killed. The provocation was not lost: the conqueror ascended a mosque, and commanded a general massacre, in which thousands were slain. Pillage accompanied murder; and whilst the streets streamed with blood, the city was fired, and the dead were consumed in the conflagration of their own habitations. If a single ray of satisfaction could be felt, amidst such a scene of horror, it must have been when Nádir commanded the steward of the wretch who was the cause of this atrocity, the infamous Sádat Khán, to send, on pain of death, an inventory of his own and his master's wealth, demanding meanwhile the two millions and a half, the original composition settled by the Nizám, from the vizier alone. Whether his "coward conscience" was alarmed at the mischief he had occasioned, or mortification at discovering that his ambition had "o'erleaped itself," and recoiled with vengeance on his own head, tempted the act, it is impossible to discover, but the guilty Sádat became his own executioner. He swallowed poison; an example followed by his steward in order to escape the rage of the offended Nádir. By the new treaty, all the western provinces, Cábul, Sind, and Múltán, were surrendered and united to Persia, and on the vernal equinox, Nádir, gorged with spoil, commenced his march from the desolated capital.

Up to this eventful era in the political history of India, the Rájpút nations had not only maintained their ground amidst the convulsions of six centuries under the paramount sway of the Islamite, but two of the three chief states, Márwár and Ambar, had by policy and valour created substantial kingdoms out of petty principalities, junior branches from which had established their independence, and still enjoy it under treaty with the British Government. Mewár at this juncture was defined by nearly the same boundaries as when Mahmúd of Ghazni invaded her in the tenth century, though her influence over many of her tributaries such as Búndi, Abu, Idar, and Deola, was destroyed. To the west, the fertile district of Godwár carried her beyond her natural barrier, the Arávalli, into the desert; while the Chambal was her limit to the east. The Kharí, separated her from Ajmír, and to the south she adjoined Málwa. These limits comprehended 130 miles of latitude and 140 of longitude, containing 10,000 towns and villages, with upwards of a millior sterling of revenue. Her chief ruled over an excellent agricultural population, and a wealthy mercantile community, and was defended by a devoted vassalage. Such was this little patriarchal state after the protracted strife which has been related ; we shall have to exhibit her, in less than half a century, on the verge of annihilation from the predatory inroads of the Mahráttas.

Having extracted *chouth* from the monarch at Delhi, the Mahráttas considered themselves entitled to make a similar demand from every subordinate principality ; and soon after taking possession of Málwa, their leader, Báji Rao, repaired to Mewár to "state his terms." The Rána desired to avoid a personal interview, and sent as his representatives the Salúmbra chief and his minister, Behári Dás. Long discussions took place as to the manner in which Báji Rao should be received, and it was settled that he should be given a seat in front of the throne—a decision which, later, formed the precedent for the position of the representative of the British Government. A treaty followed, stipulating an annual tribute of 160,000 rupees assigned to Holkár, Sindhia, and the Puár, Sindhia acting as receiver-general ; and it remained in force for ten years. This was the only tributary engagement Mewár ever entered into.

This treaty was soon followed by another event which added still further to the abasement of the Rájpúts. It will be recollected that the triple alliance formed by Rána Amra conferred on the families of Márwár and Ambar the privilege of inter-marriage with the Sesodias, with the stipulation that the issue of such marriages should enjoy the rights of primogeniture ; and the death of Jai

Singh of Ambar, two years after Nádir Shah's invasion, brought this stipulation into effect. Jai Singh's eldest son, Esúri Singh, was proclaimed Rája, though a strong party supported another son, Madhu Singh, who was nephew to the Rána of Mewár, and the lawful heir according to the treaty. Madhu Singh does not seem to have been brought up in the expectation of succeeding; and he had, with the sanction of his father, transferred his services to Mewár, where he held the fief of Rampúra. Five years elapsed before any extraordinary exertions were made to annul the rights of Esúri Singh. It would be tedious to give even an epitome of the intrigues for the accomplishment of this object, which properly belong to the annals of Ambar. The Rána took the field with his nephew, and was met by Esúri supported by the Mahráttas. But the Sesodias did not evince in the battle of Rájmahal their wonted gallantry: they were defeated and fled. The Rána vented his indignation in a galling sarcasm; he gave the sword of state to a common courtesan to carry in procession, observing "It is a woman's weapon in these degenerate days." Elated with his success, Esúri carried his resentments and his auxiliaries against the Haras of Kotah and Búndi, who had supported the cause of his antagonist. Both states suffered a diminution of territory, and were subjected to tribute by the Mahráttas. The Rána, following the example of his opponents, called in as auxiliary Malhár Rao Holkár, and engaged to pay him 64 lakhs of rupees (£800,000) on the deposal of Esúri Singh. To avoid the degradation which was now inevitable, this unfortunate prince resolved on suicide, and a dose of poison gave Madhu Singh the *gadi*, Holkár his bribe, and the Mahráttas a firm hold upon Rájasthán.

Rána Jaggat Singh died in 1752. His habits of levity and extravagance totally unfitted him for the task of governing his country at such a juncture. Like all his family, he patronised the arts. He greatly enlarged the royal palace, and spent £250,000 in embellishing the islets of the Peshola. The villas scattered over the valley were all erected by him, and many of those festivals, devoted to idleness and dissipation, and now firmly rooted in Udaipúr, were instituted by Jaggat Singh II.

Partáp II. succeeded in 1752. Of this prince history records nothing beyond the fact that the three years of his reign were marked by as many Mahrátta invasions and war contributions. He was followed by his son Ráj Singh II., who was as little entitled to the famous name he bore as had been his predecessor. During his seven years tenure of the throne, at least seven shoals of the Southrons overran Mewár, and so exhausted the country that the Rána was obliged to ask pecuniary aid from the Brahmin collector of tribute to enable him to marry the daughter of the Márwár prince. On his death, the order of succession retrograded, and devolved on his uncle Rána Arsi, who took up the reins of government in 1762.

The levity of Jaggat Singh, the inexperience of Partáp and Ráj Singh, combined with the ungovernable temper of Rána Arsi, and the circumstances under which he succeeded to power, induced a train of disorders which proved fatal to Mewár. Up to this time, mainly through the wisdom of the Pancholi ministers, not a foot of territory had been alienated. But in the calamitous times which ensued no efforts could avail to preserve the integrity of this once powerful kingdom. Factions arose, civil war broke out, and famine and pestilence once more held the land in their deadly grip. These combined evils utterly prostrated the people, and rendered them a prey to every invader until the year 1817, when they once more tasted repose under British protection.

The first limb severed from Mewár was the district of Rampúra. The ties of blood or of gratitude soon wax feeble when political expediency demands their dissolution; and Madhu Singh, finding himself firmly established on the throne of Ambar, repaid the immense sacrifices which the Rána had made to place him there by assigning the fief of Rampúra, which he had not a shadow of right to alienate, to Holkár. The latter had also become the assignee of the tribute imposed by Báji Rao, from the payment of which the Rána now justly deemed himself exempt, since it had been exacted on the understanding that no further encroachments on Mewár should be permitted. On the plea of recovering these arrears, Holkár, after many threatening letters to the Rána, advanced to the capital, and a sum of £600,000 was handed over to him before he consented to withdraw. Four years after this event, civil war broke out.

The real cause of this rebellion must ever remain a secret; for while some regard it as a patriotic effort on the part of the people to redeem themselves from foreign domination, others discover its motive in the rivalry of the hostile clans, who supported or opposed the succession of Rána Arsi. This prince is accused of having unfairly acquired the crown, by the removal of his nephew Ráj Singh; but though the traditional anecdotes of the period furnish strong grounds of suspicion, there is nothing which affords a direct confirmation of the crime. It is, however, a public misfortune when the line of succession retrogrades in Mewár. Arsi had no right to expect the inheritance he obtained, having long held a seat below the sixteen chief nobles; and as one of the "infants" (*bábas*) he had been incorporated with the second class of chieftains with an appanage of only £3,000 per annum. His defects of character had been too closely contemplated by his compeers, and had kindled too many enmities to justify the expectation that his new dignity would succeed in obliterating the memory of them; and past familiarity alone destroyed the respect to which his new position entitled him. His insolent demeanour estranged the first of the home nobility as well as the powerful clan of the Chondáwats. These chiefs formed a party to depose their sovereign, and immediately set up a youth called Ratna Singh, declared to be the posthumous son of the last Rána by the daughter of the chief of Gogúnda, though to this day disputes run high as to whether he was really the son of Ráj Singh or merely the puppet of a faction. Be the fact as it may, he was made the rallying point for the disaffected, who soon comprehended the greater portion of the nobles, while out of the "sixteen" only five withstood the defection.

The pretender took post with his faction at Komulmír, where he was formally installed, and whence he promulgated his decrees as Rána of Mewár. With that heedlessness of consequences and the political debasement which are the invariable concomitants of civil dissension, he had the meanness

Photo by] [*Donald Macbeth, London*

JAIN TEMPLE AT KOMULMÍR.

[*p.* 168

to invite Sindhia to his aid, with a promise of a reward of one million sterling on the dethronement of Arsi.

This contest introduces us to one of the most celebrated chiefs of the time, Zálim Singh of Kotah, who was destined to fill a distinguished part in the annals of Rájasthán, but more especially in Mewár, where his political sagacity first developed itself. The attack on Kotah, of which his father was military governor, first brought him into prominence, and led to an acquaintance with the Mahrátta chiefs which linked him with their policy for more than half a century. Zálim, having lost his prince's favour, whose path in love he had dared to cross, repaired, on his banishment from Kotah, to the Rána, who, observing his talents, enrolled him among his chiefs, and conferred upon him the title of Ráj Rinna, with lands for his support. By his advice, the Rána also sought the aid of the Mahráttas, one of whom he appointed to the chief office in the state, setting aside the Pancholi ministry. At this time, Madháji Sindhia was at Ujjain, and thither the conflicting parties hastened, each desirous of obtaining this chief's support. But the pretender's proposals had already been entertained, and, ere the arrival of the Rána, he was encamped with Sindhia on the banks of the Sippra.

The Rána's force, conducted by the chief of Salúmbra, the Rájas of Shápúra and Bunéra, with Zálim Singh and the Mahrátta auxiliaries, did not hesitate to attack the combined camp, and for a moment they were victorious, driving Madháji and the pretender back, with great loss, to the gates of Ujjain. Here, however, the latter rallied, and, being joined by a fresh body of troops, the battle was renewed with great disadvantage to the Rájpúts, who, deeming the day theirs, had broken and dispersed to plunder. The chiefs of Salúmbra, Shápúra, and Bunéra were slain, while Zálim Singh had his horse killed under him, and, being left wounded on the field, was made prisoner. The discomfited troops retreated to Udaipúr, while the pretender's party remained with Sindhia, inciting him to invest that capital and place Ratna on the throne. Some time, however, elapsed before he could carry this design into execution; when, at the head of a large force, the Mahrátta chief gained the passes and besieged the city. The Rána's cause now appeared hopeless. Bhím Singh of Salúmbra, uncle and successor to the chief slain at Ujjain, with the Rahtor chief of Bednor, were the only nobles of high rank who defended their prince and capital in this emergency; but the energies of a single individual saved both.

Amra Chand Barwa, of the mercantile class, had held the office of minister in the preceding reigns, when his influence had retarded the progress of evils which no human means could avert. He was now deposed; and, with a stubborn and unpopular prince, a divided aristocracy, and an impoverished country, he was little desirous of recovering his lost power. He was aware, also, of his own imperious temper, as ungovernable as that of his sovereign, but which his previous lord and master, the youthful Partáp, who regarded him as a father, had been wise enough never to check. During the ten years he had been out of office, mercenaries of Sind had been entertained and established on the forfeited lands of the clans, perpetuating discontent and stifling every latent spark of patriotism. Even those who did not join the pretender remained sullenly at their castles, and thus all confidence was annihilated. A casual incident brought Amra forward at this critical juncture. Udaipúr had neither ditch nor walls equal to its defence. Arsi was engaged in fortifying Eklingarh, a lofty hill south of the city. He was attempting to place thereon an enormous piece of ordnance, but his men were unable to get it over the craggy ascent. Amra happened to be present when the Rána arrived to inspect the proceedings. Excuses were made to avert his displeasure, when, turning to the ex-minister, he enquired what time and expense ought to attend the completion of such an undertaking. The reply was, "A few rations of grain and some days"; and he offered to accomplish the task on condition that his orders should be supreme in the valley during its performance. On his offer being accepted, he collected the whole working population, cut a road, and in a few days gave the Rána a salute from Eklingarh.

The city was now closely invested on every side but the west, where communications were still kept open by the lake, across which the mountaineers of the Arávalli, ever faithful in times of danger, kept up a constant supply of provisions. All defence rested on the fidelity of the mercenary Sindhies, and they were at this very moment insolent in their clamours for arrears of pay. Nor were the indecisive measures daily passing before their eyes calculated to augment their respect or stimulate their courage. Not satisfied with demands, they had the audacity to seize the Rána, as he entered the palace, by the skirt of his robe, which was torn in the effort to detain him. The haughtiness of his temper gave way before this humiliating proof of the hopelessness of his condition ; and while the minister counselled escape by water to the mountains, whence he might gain Mandalgarh, the Salúmbra chief confessed his inability to offer any advice save that of recourse to Amra Chand. The latter was, accordingly, summoned, and the uncontrolled charge of their desperate affairs offered to his guidance.

Amra Chand accepted the post, remarking that it was one of which no man could be covetous, and, turning to the Rána, he added: "You know also my defect of temper which admits of no control. Wherever I am, I must be absolute — no secret advisers, no counteraction of measures. With finances ruined, troops mutinous, provisions expended, if you desire me to act, swear that no order, whatever its purport, shall be countermanded, and I will try what can be done." The Rána and his chiefs bent their heads before the bold bearing of Amra, and pledged themselves by their patron deity to comply with all his requests.

Descending to the terrace where the Sindhic leaders and their bands were assembled, Amra commanded them to follow him, exclaiming, "Look to me for your arrears." The mutineers rose without reply, and in a body left the palace with Amra, who forthwith calculated the amount due, and promised payment the next day. Thence he proceeded to the repositories and, as the keepers fled when the keys of their trust were demanded, he ordered them to be broken open. All the gold and silver, whether in bullion or vessels, was converted into money; jewels were pledged, the troops paid, ammunition and provisions laid in, the enemy held at defiance, and the siege prolonged for six months.

The pretender and his party had control of all but the valley of Udaipúr; but the million pounds promised to Sindhia as the price of his aid was not forthcoming, and the impatient Mahrátta opened negotiations with Amra, offering to raise the siege and abandon the pretender for seventy lakhs of rupees. The treaty had already been signed when an exaggerated account of the wealth of the city reaching the Mahrátta's ears, he broke his faith, and demanded an additional twenty lakhs. Amra tore up the treaty, and sent back the fragments with defiance. His spirit increased with his difficulties, and he infused his gallantry into the hearts of the most despairing. Assembling the Sindhies and the home-clans who were yet true to their prince, he made known to them his negotiations with the enemy, and stirred them to enthusiasm by a spirited appeal to their courage and loyalty, while, to add weight to his words, he distributed, amongst the most deserving, jewels and other articles of ornament lying useless in the treasury. The stores of grain in the city and neighbourhood, whether public or private, were collected and sent to the market, and it was proclaimed by beat of drum, that every fighting man could have six months' provisions on application. These unexpected resources were matter of universal surprise, and especially to the besiegers. The Sindhies, having no longer cause for discontent, caught the spirit of the brave Amra, and going in a body to the palace, they paid homage to the Rána, and swore that they would defend Udaipúr to the last. The enthusiasm spread, and was announced to

Sindhia by a general discharge of cannon on his advanced posts. Apprehensive of some desperate display of Rájpút valour, the wary Mahrátta made overtures for a renewal of negotiations. It was now Amra's turn to triumph, and he replied that, so far from being able to pay ninety lakhs of rupees, he must now, to cover the expense incurred by a six months' siege, deduct ten lakhs from the amount originally demanded. Thus outwitted, Sindhia was compelled to accept sixty lakhs, with three and a half as *douceur* to the officers of his government.

Thirty-three lakhs in jewels and specie were at once made over, and lands were mortgaged for the liquidation of the remainder of the debt. These lands were never redeemed; and in 1775, when the great officers of the Mahrátta federation began to shake off the authority of the Peshwa, they became incorporated in the state of which Sindhia was the founder. Amra's defence of the capital was a death blow to the hopes of the pretender. He lost, one after another, all the strongholds he had gained in Mewár except Komulmír, whither he retired with the few chiefs who yet rallied round his standard. After a short time, these, too, abandoned him, and his cause was lost for ever.

The Rána had triumphed, but at a heavy sacrifice. The war had cost him not only the indemnity in lands and money paid to Sindhia, but the rich district of Godwár as well. This district had formed part of the territories of Mewár since the beginning of the thirteenth century, when it was won by Rahup from the prince of Mandor. During the war with the pretender, it was confided to the Rája of Jodhpur, to prevent its resources being available to the former, whose headquarters, Komulmír, commanded the approach to it, and the Rája pledged himself to support a body of 3,000 men for the Rána's service from its revenues. Arsi died soon after the war, and Godwar was never recovered.

Rana Arsi met his death by treachery. He accepted an invitation from the Hara prince of Bundi to hunt with him at the *ahairia*, or spring festival, in the course of which he was slain by the Bundi heir, at the instigation, it is said, of the Mewár nobles, who detested their prince, and with whom, since the late events, it was impossible they could ever unite in confidence. A colour of pretext was afforded to the Búndi prince by a boundary dispute regarding a patch of ground yielding only a few good mangoes; but even admitting this as a palliative, it could not justify the inhospitable act, while the mode of its execution added cowardice to barbarity. As both were pursuing the boar, the Búndi heir drove his lance through the heart of the Rána.

xv.—In the Grip of the Mahráttas

Arsi left two sons, Hamír and Bhím Singh; and in 1772, the former, still a minor, succeeded to the little enviable title of Rána. The mercenary Sindhies who, stirred to enthusiasm by Amra, had for a moment assumed the garb of fidelity, threw it off at their prince's death, and, in the temporary absence of the minister, made themselves masters of the capital. The Salúmbra chief, who had been left in charge, they imprisoned, and were about to subject him to the torture of the hot iron to extort arrears of pay, when Amra, returning unexpectedly, rescued him. The faithful minister at once set to work to restore order, and to establish the young prince firmly on his throne. But his integrity and devotion met with their inevitable reward, and he died by poison ere his work was well begun. His death yielded a flattering comment on his life; the funds he left were not sufficient to cover his funeral expenses, and he is, probably, the sole instance on record in Indian history of a minister having his obsequies defrayed by subscription among his fellow citizens.

In 1775, the queen-mother was forced to call in the aid of Sindhia to repress a rebellion of the Chondáwats. The Mahrátta recovered the crown lands which the Salúmbra had usurped, and imposed upon him a heavy fine. But instead of confining himself to the punishment of the guilty, and restoring

Photo by] [*Donald Macbeth, London*

A VIEW OF SALÚMBRA.

[*p.* 176

the lands to the young Rána, Sindhia seized the opportunity to strip the state of other fertile districts, whose annual revenues aggregated to six lakhs of rupees, and which he made over to his son-in-law and to Holkár. Besides these alienations of territory the Mahráttas levied, during the reign of Hamír, no less than seven war contributions, and inability to liquidate these exorbitant demands resulted in further sequestration of lands. Amidst such scenes of civil strife and spoliation, Hamír died before he had attained even Rájpút majority.

From the time of the first Mahrátta invasion to the death of Hamír, Mewár was despoiled of over £7,000,000 sterling. It were a waste of time to enumerate the rapacious individuals who shared the spoils of this devoted country. We may be content to say their name was legion. The Mogul princes had observed at least the forms of government and justice, which occasionally tempered their aggressions; the Mahráttas were associations of vampires, who drained the very life-blood wherever the scent of plunder attracted them. Yet the land would eventually have reimbursed even the sum just mentioned, had not the penalty inflicted for non-payment rendered the evil irremediable. The loss to the revenue through alienated lands was, at this time, more than 28 lakhs of rupees, or £323,000—more than the entire revenue of the state at the present time.

Rána Bhím Singh, with whose reign we shall bring our story of the fortunes of Mewár to a close, occupied the throne for fifty years, a period as fruitful in disaster as any that preceded it, though it paved the way to future tranquillity. The strifes that prevailed for nearly forty years after Bhím Singh's accession, group themselves round three main centres—the feud between the Chondáwats and the Suktáwats, the struggle between Ambáji and Lakwa for the vice-royalty of Sindhia's short-lived empire, and the rivalry of the princes of Márwár and Jaipúr for the hand of the Sesodia princess Kumári. These struggles dove-tail one into another with a complexity that baffles elucidation, but the same features characterise them all—intrigue, rapine, bloodshed, and devastation. The Mahráttas had gradually ceased to be a federated power. Split up into bands, each under its own leader, they roamed the country intent upon nothing but the gratification of their own lust for wealth, and utterly unscrupulous as to the means they employed. In every Rájpút dispute, the contending parties hired the assistance of one or another of these bands, to whom such employment offered every opportunity for extortion and plunder, and who generally found it to their interest to foster the quarrel they had been called in to terminate.

The feud between the two great clans began whilst Bhím Singh was still a minor. The Chondáwats had the chief control in the councils of the state, and they determined to use their power to humble their rivals. Arjan Singh was their leading warrior, and so bitter did the feud become that he mustered his kin and invested Bhíndír, the Suktáwat stronghold. Sangrám Singh, the chief of the latter clan, replied by attacking Korábar, the headquarters of Arjan's own estate. Various engagements took place, and on one occasion Arjan captured the children of Sangrám, whom he ruthlessly butchered. This act, and his own overbearing conduct in the state councils, so inflamed the queen-mother that she deprived the

Chondáwats of office, and filled their places with chieftains of the rival clan. The Chondáwats retired to Chítor, where they fortified themselves; and the Suktáwats, to strengthen their position, sought support from Zálim Singh of Kotah, who came to their aid at the head of 10,000 Mahráttas.

Such was the state of things when the ascendency of Madháji Sindhia received a severe check from the combined forces of Márwár and Jaipúr; and the battle of Lalsút, in which the Mahrátta chief was completely defeated, was the signal for the Rájpúts to resume their alienated lands. Nor was the Rána backward on this occasion, when there appeared a momentary gleam of the active virtue of past days. Nimbhahaira in the south, which had been annexed by Holkár, was first reduced, and then siege was laid to Jáwud, the governor of which, Siváji Nána, capitulated. Other districts were regained in the north, and the ancient fief of Rampúra was recovered Elated by success, the united chiefs advanced to the banks of the Rirkia, preparatory to further operations.

But the capture of Nimbhahaira drew upon them the vengeance of Ahilia Bai, the regent queen of the Holkár estate. Five thousand horse were despatched to the support of the discomfited Siváji Nána, who had taken refuge in Mandisor, where he rallied all the garrisons whom the Rájpúts had unwisely permitted to capitulate. In February 1788, the Rána's troops were surprised and defeated with great slaughter, the minister slain, and many of their chieftains captured. The newly-made conquests were rapidly lost, Jáwud being the only place which offered any show of resistance.

All the chiefs and clans of Mewár were united in

this struggle except the Chondáwats, who devoted their energies to the prosecution of their feud, and who were a source of continual trouble and danger to the queen-mother and her ministers. They still held Chítor, and their forces were constantly in collision with the troops of their rivals, while each encounter added to the general confusion and insecurity. The agriculturist, never certain of the fruits of his labours, abandoned his fields, and, at length, his country; mechanical industry found no recompense, and commerce was at the mercy of unlicensed spoliation. Hence arose a train of evils. Every cultivator sought out a patron, and entered into engagements as the price of protection. Every Rájpút possessing a horse or a lance had his clients, and not a camel-load of merchandise could pass the abode of one of these cavaliers without paying fees, while bands of Mahrátta free-booters roamed unchecked throughout the country.

The Rána and his advisers at length determined to call in Sindhia to expel the rebellious Chondáwats from the ancient capital—a step mainly prompted by Zálim Singh, who was deputed to carry the Rána's proposals to the Mahrátta chief. Since the battle of Lalsút, Sindhia had reorganised his brigades under the celebrated De Boigne, by whose assistance he had redeemed his lost influence in Rájpútána. Lalsút had been more than counterbalanced by his victories at Mairtia and Patan, where the brave Rahtors, after acts of the most devoted gallantry, were completely overthrown. Sindhia's plans coincided entirely with the object of the deputation, and he readily acquiesced in the Rána's desire A force was hastily mustered and despatched to Mewár under the Mahrátta general

Ambáji. Zálim Singh accompanied it, and they encamped before Chítor, where in a short time they were joined by Sindhia with the main body.

It is worth while to follow somewhat closely the events which followed, for they afford a characteristic picture of the diplomatic methods of the time. The three leading characters in the drama were endeavouring to compass their own several ends. Zálim's ambition, which he imagined was known only to himself, was to raise himself to a position of supreme control in Mewár. Sindhia made no secret of his motives; he wanted money to enable him to carry on his designs in the Dekhan. Ambáji's ambition was precisely the same as that of Zálim; but he was fully aware that the latter was his rival. To get rid of Zálim, whose influence he knew to be greater than his own, was therefore his immediate object, and a piece of good fortune helped him in its accomplishment.

Sindhia was anxious to receive a visit from the Rána, for even the Peshwas deemed this an honour; and to effect this object he proceeded with Zálim to Udaipúr. The chiefs met at the Tiger Mount, a few miles outside the capital, and Sindhia escorted the Rána to his camp. But in this short interval, Ambáji, who remained with the army at Chítor, entered into negotiations with the chief of the Chondáwats. He knew that Zálim was hated by the clan, and he had little difficulty in coming to terms with Bhím Singh, the Salúmbra, who agreed to surrender Chítor, to humble himself before the Rána, and to pay a contribution of twenty lakhs of rupees, provided that Zálim was ordered to quit the state. On the latter's return with the Rána, Ambáji touched on the question of Bhím Singh's surrender, "which," he casually remarked, "would be an easy matter but for your presence." Zálim, desirous of masking his own purposes, went so far as to assert that he was tired of the whole business, and that he would be only too glad if he could return to Kotah. "Is it then really your wish to retire?" asked Ambáji. "Assuredly," replied Zálim, who was much too proud to eat his own words before the Mahrátta. "Then," retorted the crafty Ambáji, "your wish shall be gratified in a few minutes;" and, giving him no time to retract, he called for his horse and galloped off to Sindhia's tent.

Zálim relied on Sindhia's not acceding to the proposition; or, if he did, that the Rána, over whom he imagined he had complete influence, would oppose it. He trusted to Sindhia for two reasons: firstly, because he had received a private promise from him that the troops left at Mewár for the restoration of order should be under his command; and secondly, because he alone was able to raise the sum stipulated for the expulsion of the Chondáwats from Chitor. But Ambáji had foreseen and provided a remedy for this latter difficulty, and upon its being urged by Sindhia, he offered himself to advance the amount by bills on the Dekhan. This argument was irresistible; money, and the consequent prosecution of his journey to Poona being within his attainment, Sindhia's engagements with Zálim and the Rána ceased to be matters of importance. He at once nominated Ambáji his lieutenant with the command of a large force, with which he would have no difficulty in reimbursing himself for the sums he had advanced. Having carried his object with Sindhia, Ambáji proceeded direct from his tent to that of the Rána, with whom, by holding out prospects of immediate peace, and by promising subserviency in all things to his wishes, he was equally successful. Having thus accomplished his purpose, he hastened back to Zálim to inform him that his wish to retire had met with general acquiescence; and so well were his arrangements made that the Rána's mace-bearer arrived at the same moment to announce that the "*khilat* of leave" awaited his acceptance.

Thus was Zálim outwitted. The Salúmbra chief descended from Chítor and "touched the Rána's feet." Sindhia pursued his march to the Dekhan, and Ambáji was left sole arbiter of Mewár. Ambáji remained eight years in Mewár, reaping its revenues, and amassing those hoards of wealth which subsequently gave him the lead in Hindustan. Yet, although he accumulated £2,000,000 from her soil, exacting one half of the produce of agricultural industry, the suppression of feuds and exterior aggressions gave to Mewár a degree of tranquillity and happiness to which she had long been a stranger. During the last year of his control, three notable events took place—the death of the queen-mother, the birth of a son and heir to the Rána, and the bursting of the embankment of the lake, which swept away a great part of the city and a third of its inhabitants.

In 1796, Sindhia appointed Ambáji his viceroy in Hindustan, and Mewár was handed over to his deputy Rai Chand. The Suktáwats still held the chief power in the state, and they never let slip an opportunity for adding to the humiliation of the

Chondáwats, many of whose fiefs they had confiscated. It was not long, however, before they quarrelled with the new deputy, and their rivals, seeing their chance, sent a deputation to Ambáji, and for the sum of ten lakhs of rupees induced the avaricious Mahrátta to withdraw his support from the Suktáwats and transfer it to themselves. In a very short time, the position of the clans was entirely reversed. The Suktáwats were driven from office, the stipulated sum of ten lakhs was raised from their estates, and the fiefs of two of their nobles were confiscated.

At this juncture, Madháji Sindhia died—an occurrence which had a material influence on the course of events in Mewár. He was succeeded by his nephew, Daulat Rao Sindhia, who was still in his minority. This latter fact added considerably to the powers of Ambáji, though his position had suddenly become insecure owing to the appearance of a rival competitor for the viceroyalty in the person of Lakwa Dáda, who had support of the Madháji's family. Mewár had the misfortune to be the arena on which the rival satraps contested their claims. Lakwa wrote to the Rána commanding him to throw off Ambáji's yoke, and expel his deputy; while Ambáji instructed his deputy to eject every supporter of Lakwa, from the state. The chiefs declared for Lakwa, and Siváji Nána hastened from Jáwud with all the troops he could collect to support the deputy. Things went badly with Nána at first, and he was obliged to barricade himself in the fortress of Hamírgarh, which Lakwa immediately invested. But reinforcements were soon at hand. Bala Rao, Ambáji's brother, came at the head of a large body of infantry and artillery and was joined on the march by Zálim Singh of Kotah with his auxiliaries. Lakwa was forced to raise the siege and to retire to Kadúra on the banks of the Banás, where he encamped for the rainy season. Nána and his auxiliaries abandoned their stronghold and took up their quarters at Amli, also on the banks of the Banás, and almost in sight of Lakwa's camp. By this time Nána had been still further reinforced by a detachment under the celebrated soldier of fortune, George Thomas. Ten miles north of Amli was the town of Shápúra, whose chief, one of the few nobles of Mewár who sided against Lakwa, procured supplies for Nána's force.

For six weeks the two armies faced one another. The chiefs of Mewár hovered around Nána's camp to cut off his supplies; but Thomas escorted the convoys from Shápúra with his regulars and defied all their efforts. At length the monsoon ceased, and Thomas advanced his batteries against Lakwa. A general assault was about to be made by the whole of Nána's forces when there came on a terrific storm, with torrents of rain, which filled the stream across which Thomas had just advanced his guns, and cut them off from the main body. So tremendous was the force of the elements that Shápúra, over which the storm burst, was laid in ruins. Lakwa seized the moment, and, with the Mewár chiefs, stormed and carried the isolated batteries, capturing fifteen pieces of cannon; while the Shápúra chief, threatened at once by his brother nobles and the vengeance of heaven, refused further provision to Nána, who was compelled to abandon his position and retreat to Sanganar.

The discomfited general vowed vengeance against the estates of the Mewár chieftains, and after a short time, being reinforced by Ambáji, again took the field. Then commenced scenes of carnage and pillage such as even Mewár had seldom witnessed. The whole of the Chondáwat estates under the Arávalli range were laid waste, the castles of the chiefs were assaulted, many taken and destroyed, and heavy sums levied on all. Whilst the work of destruction was still proceeding, Ambáji was dispossessed of the government of Hindustan, and Lakwa appointed in his place. The struggle was, therefore, at an end, and Nána was compelled to surrender all the fortresses and towns he held in Mewár. Lakwa showed his gratitude for the assistance he had received by exacting a contribution of 24 lakhs from the state, which he collected by force of arms. He then set out for Jaipúr, leaving Jaswant Rao Bhao behind as his deputy. The Chondáwats were again in power, the Rána, a large portion of whose personal domain they appropriated to themselves, being little more than a tool in their hands.

xvi.—Ruin and Rescue

WHILST his satraps were thus contending for the viceroyalty of Hindustan, Daulat Rao Sindhia was pursuing his schemes against Holkár for the supremacy of the Dekhan, and the British were gradually preparing to extinguish the whole mighty conflagration. The battle of Indore in 1802, where 150,000 men were assembled to dispute the claims to the predatory empire, wrested the ascendency from Holkár, who lost his guns, his equipage, and his capital. He fled to Mewár, plundering Ratlám on his way, and was only prevented from visiting Udaipúr by the rapidity of Sindhia's pursuit. He pushed on to Nathdwára, about 25 miles north of Udaipúr, and the shrine of the Hindu Apollo. It was here that this active soldier first showed signs of mental derangement. He upraided Krishna while prostrate before his image for the loss of victory, and levied three lakhs of rupees on the priests of the temple and the inhabitants of the town. Fearing that the portal of the god would prove no bar to the impious Mahrátta, the high priest caused the deity to be removed from his pedestal, and sent him with his establishment to Udaipúr. The chief of Kotário, in whose estate the sacred fane was situated, undertook the escort, and conveyed the image through intricate passes to the capital. On his return he was intercepted by a band of Holkár's troops who demanded the surrender of his horses. But the chief was the descendant of the illustrious Prithvi Ráj, and preferred death to dishonour. Dismounting, he hamstrung his steed, and, commanding his retainers to do the same, advanced on foot against his enemies. The conflict was short and unequal, and the Kontário, with all his gallant band, fell sword in hand.

Holkár pursued his way to Ajmír, and thence to Jaipúr. Sindhia's leaders, on reaching Mewár, renounced the pursuit, and for some days Udaipúr was cursed with their presence, when three lakhs of rupees were extorted from the unfortunate Rána, raised by the sale of household effects and the jewels of the females of his family.

Two years later, Holkár, having recruited his shattered forces, again left the south and entered Mewár, bent on vengeance for the non-compliance with his demands for money and assistance during his retreat after the battle of Indore. The rivalry of the clans had prevented any attempt on the part of the Rána or his ministers to recuperate the strength of the state. The Chondáwats had the upper hand, and it was their ambassador, Ajít Singh, who was sent to meet the Mahrátta as he approached Udaipúr. The demand which was made was for no less a sum than 40 lakhs of rupees, or £500,000, of which one third was commanded to be instantly forthcoming. The palace was denuded of whatever could be converted into money; the females were deprived of every article of luxury and comfort; while hostages from the households of the Rána and the chief citizens were delivered as security for the remainder, and were immured in Holkár's camp.

Having spent nearly eight months in his work of extortion, Holkár was about to depart, when the arrival of Sindhia in Mewár caused him to alter his plans. The hatchet was temporarily buried between these two predatory potentates, both of whom, in their efforts to cope with the British power, had suffered heavy losses and humiliation, and they now met to concert a joint plan of campaign against their common enemy. During the rainy season of 1805, both armies encamped in the plains of Mewár, desirous, but afraid, to seek revenge in the renewal of the war. Deprived of all power in Hindustan, and of their choicest territories north and south of the Narbadda, and each with a numerous and discontented army, inflamed by defeat and clamouring for pay, they had no alternative but to pacify their soldiery and replenish their own resources by indiscriminate pillage. The horrors that befell the defenceless state are indescribable, while the position was rendered still more hopeless by the return to India of Lord Cornwallis, and the consequent resumption by the British of the policy of "non-interference," which left these insatiable freebooters to continue their depredations unchecked.

The Mahrátta leaders had taken up their quarters in the district of Bednor, about ninety-six miles north of the capital, and their respective camps, some twenty miles distant from each other, became the rendezvous of the rival clans. Sirdar Singh, the organ of the Chondáwats, represented the Rána at the court of Sindhia, at the head of whose councils was Ambáji, who had succeeded in displacing his late antagonist, Lakwa. But Ambáji had not forgotten the part played by Mewár in his downfall; and, with a view to satisfying his revenge, he now counselled the partition of the state between the Mahrátta leaders.

But whilst his baneful influence was preparing this result, the credit of Sangrám, the Suktáwat leader, with Holkár counteracted it. Even the hostile clans stifled their animosities when Ambáji's schemes became known, and Sirdar Singh left Sindhia's camp, and joined Sangrám with Holkár. Together with the minister, the upright Kishen Dás, they went before Holkár and demanded to know if he had given his consent to sell Mewár to Sindhia. Touched by the distress of the Rána and his country, Holkár swore it should not be; he counselled them to unity amongst themselves, and caused the representatives of the rival clans to "eat opium together." Nor did he stop here, but with the envoys repaired to Sindhia's tents, where he descanted on the Rána's high descent, urging that it did not become them to overwhelm him, and that they should even renounce the mortgaged lands which their fathers had too long unjustly held, himself setting the example by the restitution of Nimbhahaira. To strengthen his argument, he expatiated with Sindhia on the policy of conciliating the Rána, whose strongholds might be available in the event of a renewal of hostilities with the British. Sindhia appeared to convert to his views, and retained the envoys in his camp.

During the next few days incessant torrents of rain fell and prevented all intercourse between the courts. In this interim Holkár received information that an envoy of the Rána was in Lord Lake's camp negotiating for the aid of the British troops, then at Tonk, to drive the Mahráttas from Mewár. Sending for the Rána's ambassadors, he assailed them with a torrent of reproach; accusing them of treachery, he threw the paper containing the information at Kishen Dás, asking if that were the way in which a Rájpút kept his faith. "I shrank not," he said, "from risking Sindhia's enmity by supporting your master; and now, in combating the Faringhis, when all Hindus should be as brothers, your sovereign the Rána, who boasts of never acknowledging the supremacy of Delhi, is the first to make terms with them. Was it for this that I prevented Ambáji being fastened on you?" Kishen Dás attempted an explanation, but Holkár would hear none. Scenting danger on all sides, he determined to quit Mewár forthwith, though he had the generosity to stipulate, before his departure, for the security of the Rána and his country, telling Sindhia he should hold him personally responsible if the prince's independence were compromised. He crossed the boundary northward; but his sins were too great for even the policy of non-interference to cover. He was encountered and pursued to the Punjab by the British under the intrepid and enterprising Lake, and forced into submission at the altars of Alexander. Sindhia paid little attention to Holkár's warning, and a contribution of sixteen lakhs was at once levied on Mewár, and a brigade under Baptiste was detached from his camp for the purpose of enforcing payment.

It would be imagined that the miseries of Rána Bhím were not susceptible of aggravation, and that fortune had done her worst to humble him; but his pride as a sovereign and his feelings as a parent were destined to be yet more deeply outraged. Almost at the same time as the departure of Holkár, there arrived at Udaipúr a detachment of the troops of Jaipúr, bringing proposals for the marriage of their prince with the Rána's daughter. The Jaipúr *cortège* encamped near the capital, and the Rána's acknowledgments and acceptance of the proposal were despatched to Jaipúr. But Rája Mán of Márwár also advanced pretensions to the hand of the princess, on the ground that she had been actually betrothed to his predecessor. She had been betrothed, he said, to the throne of Márwár, not to the individual occupant; and he vowed resentment and opposition if his claims were disregarded.

Krishna Kumári was the name of the lovely object, rivalry for whose hand assembled under the banners of her admirers, Jaggat Singh of Jaipúr and Rája Mán of Márwár, not only their native chivalry, but all the predatory powers of Hindustan. Sindhia, having been denied a pecuniary demand by Jaipúr, opposed the nuptials, and aided the claims of Rája Mán by demanding of the Rána the dismissal of the Jaipúr embassy. This being refused, he advanced his brigades and batteries; and, after repulsing a fruitless resistance, in which the troops of Jaipúr joined, he forced the pass into the valley of Udaipúr with a corps of 8,000 men, and encamped within cannon range of the city. The Rána had no alternative but to dismiss the nuptial *cortége*, and agree to whatever was demanded. Sindhia remained a month in the valley, during which an interview took place between him and the Rána at the shrine of Eklinga. To increase his importance, the Mahrátta invited the British envoy and his staff, who had just arrived at his camp, to be present on the occasion. The princely bearing of the Rána and his sons made a great impression on the visitors, being in marked contrast

Photo by] RÁJPÚT LADY AND WARRIOR. [*Donald Macbeth, London*

[p. 192

to that of the Mahrátta and his suite;[1] while the regal abode of this ancient race acted with irresistible force on the cupidity of Sindhia, who aspired to, yet dared not, seat himself in "the palace of the Cæsars." It was even surmised that his hostility to Jaipúr was not so much from the refused war-contribution as from a mortifying negative to his own proposal for the hand of the Mewár princess.

The heralds of Hymen being thus rudely repulsed, the Jaipúr prince prepared to avenge his insulted pride and disappointed hopes, and, accordingly, arrayed a force such as had not assembled in Hindustan since the empire was in its glory. Rája Mán eagerly took up the gauntlet, and headed the "swords of Maru." But dissension prevailed in Márwár, where rival claimants for the throne had divided the loyalty of the clans, introducing there also the influence of the Mahráttas. The marriage proposals gave the malcontents an opportunity for displaying their long curbed resentments, and, following the example of Mewár, they set up a pretender, whose interests were eagerly espoused, and whose standard was erected in the array of Jaipúr. A battle was fought at Parbatsír on the common boundary of the two states; but the action was short, for while a heavy cannonade opened on both sides, the majority of the Márwár nobles went over to the pretender. Rája Mán turned his poniard against himself, but some chiefs yet faithful to him wrested the weapon from his hand, and conveyed him from the field. He was pursued to his capital, which was invested and gallantly defended during six months. The town was at length taken and plundered; but the castle

[1] Colonel Tod was himself present at this interview.

of Joda defied every assault, and in time the mighty host of Jaipúr, which had eaten the country bare for twenty miles round, began to crumble away: intrigue spread through its ranks, and the siege ended in pusillanimity and flight. Jaggat Singh, humbled and crestfallen, skulked from the desert retreat of his rival, indebted to a partisan corps for safety and convoy to his capital, around whose walls the wretched remnants of his ill-starred troops long lagged in expectation of pay, while the bones of their horses whitened the plain on every side.

Rája Mán owed his delivery to one of the most notorious villains that India ever produced, the Nawáb Amír Khán. This man held command of a brigade of artillery and horse in Jaipúr's army, but in the course of the siege he deserted to the side of Márwár; and he now offered, for a specific sum, to rid the Rája of the pretender and all his associates. The offer was accepted, and Amír Khán was not long in laying his plans. Like Judas he kissed whom he betrayed. He took service with the pretender, and, at a shrine of a saint of his own faith, exchanged turbans with his leaders, a ceremony equivalent to the most solemn oath of friendship. The too credulous Rájpúts celebrated this acquisition to their party by feasting and revelry; but in the midst of dance and song, the tents were cut down, and the victims, enveloped in their toils, were slaughtered by the Khán's followers with showers of grape.

Thus finished the under-plot; but another, and more noble, victim was demanded before discomfited ambition could repose, or the curtain drop on this eventful drama. Neither party would relinquish his claim to the fair object of the war; and it was the unhallowed suggestion of the same ferocious Khán that the blood of the princess could alone extinguish the torch of discord. We need not analyse the motives that prompted him to this devilish scheme. He had determined to make himself all-powerful in Márwár, and the alliance of Rája Mán with Mewár was not calculated to further his object; nor was he anxious for a renewal of the war with Jaipúr, which he knew to be inevitable unless the dispute were settled. Through the medium of the Chondáwat, Ajít, whom a heavy bribe had made his accomplice, he revealed his design to the Rána, and induced him to believe that there were but two alternatives to his daughter's death. Either he must force her, already promised to the Jaipúr prince, into a dishonourable marriage with Rája Mán, or, by refusing to do so, draw ruin upon himself and his country. The fiat was passed that Krishna Kumári should die.

Krishna Kumári Bai, the "virgin princess Krishna," was in her sixteenth year. Her mother was of the Cháwura race, descended from the ancient kings of Anhulwára. Sprung from the noblest blood of Hind, Kumári added beauty of face and form to an engaging demeanour, and was justly celebrated as "the flower of Rájasthán." When the fatal cup was presented to her she received it with a smile, at the same time addressing words of comfort to her frantic mother; "Why afflict yourself, my mother, at this shortening of the sorrows of life? I fear not to die. We are marked out for sacrifice from our birth; let me thank my father that I have lived so long." Three times the nauseating draught failed in its object. A fourth, a powerful opiate, was prepared and administered, and "the desires of barbarity were accomplished. She slept." The wretched mother did not long survive her child; nature was exhausted in the ravings of despair; she refused food, and in a few days her remains followed those of Kumári to the funeral pyre.

Even the Khán, when the instrument of his infamy, Ajít, reported the issue, could not conceal his contempt, and tauntingly asked "if this were the boasted Rájpút valour." But a yet sterner rebuke awaited the dishonoured Chondáwat. Four days after the crime had been committed, Sangrám reached the capital—a man in every respect the reverse of Ajít. Audaciously brave, the chief of the Suktáwats feared neither the frown of his sovereign nor the sword of his enemy. Without introduction he made his way into the presence. "O dastard!" he exclaimed, "thou hast thrown dust on the Sesodia race; thou hast defiled by thy sin the blood which has flowed in purity for a hundred ages. Let no Sesodia ever hold up his head again! The line of Bappa Ráwul is at an end. Heaven has ordained this, a signal for our destruction." Then, turning upon Ajít, who was present, he continued: "Thou stain on the Sesodia race, thou impure of Rájpút blood, dust be on thy head as thou hast covered us all with shame. May you die childless, and your name die with you."

The traitor to manhood and his sovereign dared no reply. Sangrám died not long afterwards, but his curse was fulfilled. The Rána had ninety-five children; but only one of his sons grew to manhood, and only two daughters reached the marriageable age. The latter were united to the princes of

Jaisalmír and Bíkanír, in which states the Salic law precludes all honour through female descent. With regard to Ajít, the curse was fully accomplished. Scarcely a month after it was uttered, his wife and two sons died. The traitor himself wandered from shrine to shrine performing penance, his beads in his hand, and *Ráma! Ráma!* ever on his lips. But enough of him! Let us dismiss him with the words of Sangrám, "dust on his head."

The mind sickens at the contemplation of these unvarying scenes of atrocity; but this unhappy state had yet to pass through two more lustres of aggravated sufferings. From the day when the embassy of Jaipúr was expelled, that of the British was in the train of Sindhia, a witness to the evils described, but powerless to offer protection. In the spring of 1806, when the embassy entered Mewár, nothing but ruin met the eye—deserted towns, roofless houses, and uncultivated plains. Wherever the Mahrátta encamped, annihilation was ensured—it was a habit—and twenty-four hours sufficed to give the most flourishing spot the aspect of a desert. His march was always to be traced for days afterwards by burning villages and destroyed cultivation.

Some satisfaction may result from the fact that there was scarcely an actor in these scenes whose end was not fitted to his career. Ambáji was compelled to disgorge the spoils of Mewár, and his personal sufferings made some atonement for the ills he had inflicted on her. This satrap, who had almost established his independence in the fortress and territory of Gwalior, suffered every indignity from Sindhia. He was confined in a mean tent, manacled, and suffered the torture of small lighted torches applied to his fingers. He attempted suicide to avoid the surrender of his riches, but the instrument, a small English penknife, was insufficient for his purpose. The surgeon to the British embassy sewed up the wounds, and his coffers were eased of fifty-five lakhs of rupees. He died shortly after, and, if report be correct, the residue of his treasure was possessed by his ancient ally, Zálim Singh.

In 1809, Amír Khán led his myrmidons to the capital, threatening the demolition of the shrine of Eklinga if refused a contribution of eleven lakhs of rupees. Nine were agreed to, but by no effort could the sum be raised; whereupon the Rána's envoys were treated with indignity, and Kishen Dás, the minister, wounded. The passes to the valley of Udaipúr were again forced, Amír Khán entering by Dobári, and his son-in-law, the notorious Jamshíd, by Chirwa. Their ruffianly Patháns were billeted on the city, which still bears traces of the barbarities they committed. In 1811, Bappu Sindhia arrived with the title of Subhadár, and encamped in the valley, and from this to 1814 these vampires possessed themselves of the entire fiscal domain, with many of the fiefs, often disputing with each other over the spoils. Mewár was fast approaching dissolution. Her fields were lying fallow, her cities in ruins, her inhabitants exiled, her chieftains demoralised, and her prince and his family destitute of the common comforts of life. But deliverance was at hand. In 1813, the Marquis of Hastings succeeded Lord Cornwallis as Governor-General of India, and the vigorous policy of Lord Wellesley was at once resumed. The Mahráttas were everywhere defeated, and in 1817

Mewár, in company with nearly every state in Rájpútána, passed under the protecting arm of Great Britain.

The articles of the treaty which was entered into were ten in number, and were as follows :—

TREATY between the Honourable the English East India Company and Maharana Bhim Singh, Rana of Oudeepoor, concluded by Mr Charles Theophilus Metcalf on the part of the Honourable Company, in virtue of full powers granted by his Excellency the Most Noble the Marquis of Hastings, K.G., Governor-General, and by Thakoor Ajeet Sing on the part of the Maharana, in virtue of full powers confirmed by the Maharana aforesaid.

First Article.—There shall be perpetual friendship, alliance, and unity of interests between the two states, from generation to generation, and the friends and enemies of one shall be the friends and enemies of both.

Second Article.—The British Government engages to protect the principality and territory of Oudeepoor.

Third Article.—The Maharana of Oudeepoor will always act in subordinate co-operation with the British Government, and acknowledge its supremacy, and will not have any connection with other chiefs or states.

Fourth Article.—The Maharana of Oudeepoor will not enter into any negotiation with any chief or state without the knowledge and sanction of the British Government; but his usual amicable correspondence with friends and relations shall continue.

Fifth Article.—The Maharana of Oudeepur will not commit aggressions upon any one; and if by accident a dispute arise with any one, it shall be submitted to the arbitration and award of the British Government.

Sixth Article.—One-fourth of the revenue of the actual territory of Oudeepur shall be paid annually to the British

Government as tribute for five years; and after that term three-eighths in perpetuity. The Maharana will not have connection with any other power on account of tribute, and if any one advance claims of that nature, the British Government engages to reply to them.

Seventh Article.—Whereas the Maharana represents that portions of the dominions of Oudeepur have fallen, by improper means, into the possession of others, and solicits the restitution of those places: the British Government from a want of accurate information is not able to enter into any positive engagement on this subject; but will always keep in view the renovation of the prosperity of the state of Oudeepur, and after ascertaining the nature of each case, will use its best exertions for the accomplishment of the object, on every occasion on which it may be proper to do so. Whatever places may thus be restored to the state of Oudeepur by the aid of the British Government, three-eighths of their revenues shall be paid in perpetuity to the British Government.

Eighth Article.—The troops of the state of Oudeepur shall be furnished according to its means, at the requisition of the British Government.

Ninth Article.—The Maharana of Oudeepur shall always be absolute ruler of his own country, and the British jurisdiction shall not be introduced into that principality.

Tenth Article.—The present treaty of ten articles having been concluded at Dihlee, and signed and sealed by Mr Charles Theophilus Metcalfe and Thakoor Ajeet Sing Bahadoor, the ratifications of the same, by his Excellency the Most Noble the Governor-General, and Maharana Bheem Sing, shall be mutually delivered within a month from this date.

Done at Dihlee, this thirteenth day of January, A.D. 1818.

(*Signed*) C. T. METCALFE (L.S.)
THAKOOR AJEET SING (L.S.)

xvii.—After the Treaty

It only remains to give a brief sketch of the manner in which, under the ægis of Great Britain, the restoration of Mewár to prosperity was effected. The picture is one well worthy of study, and particularly by those who are inclined to belittle or ignore the benefits which British rule has conferred upon the subject races of India, or who profess to believe that the permanence of that rule is not essential to their future progress and welfare. The suffering, bloodshed, and oppression described in the previous chapters were not confined to the state of Mewár. They prevailed to a similar extent in every principality in Rájasthán: it is hardly an exaggeration to say they prevailed throughout the length and breadth of India.

The destruction of that vast predatory system, under the weight of which the prosperity of these regions had been so long repressed, was effected in 1817 in one short campaign. To prevent its recurrence, it was deemed politic to unite all these settled states in one grand confederation. Accordingly, the Rájpút princes were invited to shelter under our protecting alliance, and they eagerly embraced the invitation. The ambassadors of the various governments followed each other to Delhi where the treaties were negotiated, and in a few weeks all Rájpútána was united to Britain by compacts similar to that we have already quoted, ensuring to them external protection with internal independence, as the price of acknowledged supremacy, and a portion of revenue to the protecting government.

Of all the princes who obtained succour at this momentous crisis in the political history of India, none stood more in need of it than the Rána of Udaipúr. On the 15th of January 1818, the treaty was signed, and, in February, an envoy was nominated, who immediately proceeded to the Rána's court to superintend and maintain the newly-formed relations. The right wing of the grand army had already preceded him to compel the surrender of such territory as was unjustly held by the lawless partisans of Sindhia. Raipúr, Rájnaggar, and other alienated districts soon surrendered, and the payment of the arrears of the garrison put Komulmír once more in the possession of Mewár. During the march from Jaházpúr on the eastern boundary to Komulmír in the west, a distance of 140 miles, only two thinly populated towns were seen which acknowledged the Rána's authority. All was desolate. The *babul* and the gigantic reed which harboured the boar and the tiger, grew upon the highways, and every rising ground displayed a mass of ruin. Bhilwára, the commercial *entrepôt* of Rájpútána, which ten years before contained 6,000 families, was a city of the dead. No living thing appeared in her streets except a solitary dog that fled in dismay from its lurking place in the temple, scared at the unaccustomed sight of man.

The prince Javan Singh, with all the state insignia, and a numerous retinue, advanced to Nathdwára to conduct the mission to the capital. A spot was selected in a grove of palmyras, about two miles from the city, where carpets were spread; and there the prince received the Agent and his suite. His bearing was courteous and dignified; indeed, it might have been said of him, as Jahángír said of the son of Rána Amra, that "his countenance carried the impression of his illustrious extraction." We[1] entered the city by the "gate of the sun," and, through a vista of ruin, the mission was escorted to its future residence. Like all the mansions of Rájpútána, it was a quadrangular pile, with an open courtyard, and suites of apartments on each of its sides. On our arrival here, a second deputation arrived from the Rána to welcome us to his capital, bearing 100 trays of sweatmeats and drieds fruits, and a purse of 1,000 rupees for distribution among the domestics. The following day was fixed for our reception at the court of the prince.

At four in the afternoon, a deputation consisting of the officiating prime minister, the representative of the Chondáwats, with mace-bearers and a numerous escort, came to announce the Rána's readiness to receive the mission. The procession, with all the "pomp and circumstance" peculiar to these states, was marshalled in front of the Residency, the grounds of which were thronged with gaily dressed spectators, silently gazing at the unusual sight. The grand *nakarras* having announced the Rána in his court, the mission proceeded to the palace, through streets which everywhere presented signs of rapine, but hailed by the most enthusiastic greetings. "*Ji! Ji! Faringhi ká Ráj*" (Victory, victory to the English Government), resounded from every tongue. The bards were not idle; and the unpoetic name of

[1] Colonel Tod was the Agent in charge of the mission.

the Agent was hitched into rhyme. Groups of musicians were posted here and there, who gave a passing specimen of the *tuppas* of Mewár, and not a few of the fair, with brazen ewers of water on their heads, welcomed us with the *suhailia*, or song of joy. Into each of these vessels, the purse-bearer dropped a piece of silver; for neither the *suhailia* nor the *tuppas* of the minstrels are to be received without acknowledgment. As we ascended the main streets leading to the *tripolia*, or triple portal, which guards the sacred enclosure, dense masses of people blocked our progress; and even the walls of the temple of Jaggarnáth were crowded. According to etiquette, we dismounted at the gate, and proceeded on foot across the ample terrace, on which were being paraded the Rána's horses and state elephants.

The palace is a most imposing pile, of a regular form, built of granite and marble, rising at least 100 feet from the ground, and flanked with octagonal towers, crowned with cupolas. Although built at various periods, its uniformity of design has been very well preserved; nor is there in the east a more striking or majestic structure. It stands upon the very crest of a ridge running parallel to, but considerably elevated above, the margin of the lake. The terrace, which is at the east and front of the building, extends throughout its length, and is supported by a triple row of arches rising one above the other from the declivity of the ridge. The height of this arcaded wall is fully 50 feet; and although all is hollow beneath, yet so admirable is its construction that the royal stables are built on the extreme verge of the terrace, on which the

Photo by] THE PALACE OF UDAIPUR. [*Donald Macbeth, London*

[p. 204

whole personal force of the Rána, horse, foot, and elephants, are often assembled.

A band of Sindhies guarded the first entrance to the palace, while the Suktáwats were on duty in the great hall of assembly. We proceeded through lines of Rájpúts till we came to the marble staircase, where an image of Ganesh, the elephant god, guarded the ascent to the interior of the palace. After traversing a number of apartments, each filled with spectators, the herald's voice announced to "the lord of the world" that the English envoy was in his presence, whereon he arose, and advanced a few paces in front of the throne, the chiefs by whom he was surrounded standing. The apartment chosen for the visit was the Surya Mahal, or "hall of the sun," so called from a medallion of the orb in *basso reliévo* which decorates the wall. Close thereto was the Rána's throne, above which was a velvet canopy supported on slender silver columns. The seat allotted to the envoy was immediately in front of, and touching, the royal cushion. The chiefs of the higher grade, or "the sixteen," were seated according to their rank on the right and left of the Rána, and below these were the two princes Amra and Javan Singh. At either end of the front row, and at right angles to it, were the chiefs of the second rank. The civil officers of the state were near the Rána in front, and the seneschal, the keeper of the wardrobe, and other confidential officers and inferior chieftains, formed a group standing on the extreme edge of the carpet.

The Rána's congratulations were hearty and sincere; in a few powerful expressions he depicted the miseries he had experienced, the fallen condition of his state, and the gratitude he felt to the British Government which had interposed between him and destruction; and which for the first moment of his existence allowed him to sleep in peace. There was an intense earnestness in every word he uttered, which, delivered with fluency of speech and dignity of manner, inspired deep respect and sympathy. The Agent said that the Governor-General was no stranger to the history of his illustrious family, or his own immediate sufferings; and that it was his earnest desire to promote, by every means in his power, the Rána's personal dignity and the prosperity of his dominions After a few moments' conversation, the interview was closed with presents to the Agent and suite: to the former a caparisoned elephant and horse, jewelled aigrette, and pearl necklace, and to the latter shawls and brocades. The customary presentation of essence of rose and the *pán* leaf was then made, and, the Rána having risen, the Agent made his *salaam* and retired.

In a short time the Rána, attended by his second son, ministers, and a select number of the chiefs, paid a return visit. The Agent advanced beyond his residence to meet the prince, who was received with presented arms by the guard, the officers saluting, and conducted to his throne, which had been previously arranged. Conversation was unrestrained, and questions were demanded regarding everything which appeared unusual. After sitting half an hour, the Agent presented to the Rána an elephant and two horses, caparisoned with silver and guilt ornaments and velvet embroidered housings, with twenty-one shields[1] of shawls, brocades, muslins,

[1] The buckler is the tray in which gifts are presented by the Rájpúts.

and jewels; to prince Amra, unable from sickness to attend his father, a horse and eleven shields; to his brother, the second prince, Javan Singh, a horse and nine shields; and to the ministers and chiefs according to rank: the whole entertainment costing about 20,000 rupees, or £2,000.

The restoration of order out of the chaos which prevailed was no light undertaking. The institutions of the state had been reduced to a dead letter; the nobles were demoralised and rebellious, the prince's authority was despised, internal commerce abandoned, and the peasantry ruined by the combined effects of war, pestilence, and exile. The valley of the capital was the only part of Mewár over which the Rána's sway was anything more than nominal; and though Chítor and Mandalgarh were maintained by the fidelity of his servants, their revenues scarcely sufficed to provide for their garrisons. The Rána himself was mainly indebted to Zálim Singh of Kotah for the means of subsistence; for, in the general confusion and distress, the chiefs thought only of themselves, of defending their own estates, or buying off their foes; while those who succumbed took to horse, scoured the country, and plundered without distinction. Feuds multiplied, and the name of each clan inspired alarm or defiance in its neighbours. The Bhíls descended from their forests, and planted ambuscades for the traveller and merchant, whom they carried to their retreats, where they languished in durance till ransomed; and the Rájpút scrupled not to associate, and to divide the spoil, with these lawless tribes.

The capital will serve as a specimen of the country. Udaipúr, which formerly reckoned 50,000 houses within its walls, had now less than 3,000 occupied; the rest were in ruin, the rafters being taken for firewood. The realisation of the spring harvest of 1818, from the entire fiscal land, was about £4,000. Grain sold for seven seers the rupee, though thrice that quantity was procurable within a distance of 80 miles. Insurance for merchandise from the capital to Nathdwára, a distance of 25 miles, was eight per cent. of the value. The Kotário chief, whose ancestors are immortalised for their fidelity, had not a horse to conduct him to his prince's presence, though the annual value of his estates was 50,000 rupees. The Rána, the descendant of those patriotic Rájpúts who opposed Bábar, Akbar, and Aurangzeb, in the days of Mogul splendour, had not fifty horse to attend him, and was indebted, as we have already told, for the common necessities of life to the liberality of Kotah.

But the elements of prosperity, though scattered, were not extinct; and recollections of the past, deeply engraven on the minds of the people, were available to reanimate their moral and physical existence. To recall these was the main object to which the efforts of the mission were directed, and moral persuasion was the chief, if not the sole, means employed in its accomplishment. The lawless free-booter, and even the savage Bhíl, felt awed at the agency of a power never seen. To such men moral force was incomprehensible, and they attributed its results to another agency—magic; and the belief was current throughout the intricate regions of the west, that a single British officer could carry an army in his pocket, and that his power could animate slips of paper cut into the figures of armed men, from which no precautions could guard their retreats. Accordingly, at the mere name of the British power, rapine ceased, and the chieftains of the mountain wilds, who had hitherto laughed at subjection, to the number of 700, put each the sign of the dagger to a treaty, promising abstinence from plunder and a return to industrious life. In Rájpútána, the moral effect of beholding a Peshwa marched into exile with all the quietude of a pilgrimage, accomplished more than 20,000 bayonets, and no other auxiliary was required than the judicious use of the impressions from this and other passing events to relay the foundations of order and prosperity. By never doubting the issue, success was ensured. The British force was, therefore, after the execution of the plans enumerated, marched to cantonments; the rest was left for time and reason to accomplish.

One of the main obstacles to rapid progress was the inefficiency of the civil officers of the government. There seemed to be neither talent, influence, nor honesty, left in Mewár. The Rána's character was little calculated to supply the deficiencies of his officers. Though perfectly versed in the past history of his country, and possessed of ability, learning, and sound judgment, his powers were almost completely nullified by his weak points. Vain displays, frivolous amusements, and an ill-regulated liberality were all that occupied him; and, so long as he could gratify these propensities, he trusted complacently to the exertions of others for the restoration of his authority. The only man of integrity and efficiency about the court was Kishen

Dás, who had long acted as ambassador, and to his assiduity the sovereign and the country owed much; but his services were soon cut short by death.

The first point secured was the recognition of the prince's authority by his nobles, the surest signs of which were their frequent visits to the capital, where some had never been, and others only when it suited their convenience or their plans. In a few weeks, the Rána saw himself surrounded by a court such as had not been known for half a century. The recall of the exiled population was a work requiring more time; for many had formed ties or incurred obligations amongst the communities that had sheltered them, and these could not be at once disengaged or annulled. But innumerable proofs were forthcoming that neither oppression from without nor tyranny within could obliterate the feeling for the *bapota*, "the land of their fathers." What their deliverance meant to these people only those who had witnessed the day of trouble, and beheld the progress of desolation—the standing corn grazed by Mahrátta horse, the rifled towns devoted to the flames, the cattle driven to the hostile camp, the elders of the village seized as hostages for money never to be raised—could realise. To be permitted to see these evils banished, to behold the survivors of oppression congregated from the most distant provinces, awaiting with their aged and helpless the "lucky day" to take possession of their ruined abodes, was a pleasure which memory will not part with. On the 3rd of Sáwun (July), 300 people marched into the village of Kupásan, close to the capital. They were accompanied by their waggons and implements of labour, and preceded by banners and music. Ganesh[1] was once more evoked as they reconsecrated their dwellings, and placed his picture as the guardian of their portals. On the same day, and within eight months of the signing of the treaty, above 300 towns and villages were re-inhabited; and the land which had for many years been a stranger to the plough was broken up. Well might the superstitious imagine that miracles were abroad; for even to those who watched the work in progress—habitations covering the waste, the verdant corn springing up where but lately they had roused the boar from his retreat—the result was little short of magical. It was a day of pride for Britain. By such exertions of her power in distant lands is her sway hallowed.

The settlement of feudal rights was the most difficult and delicate task of all. Feuds had to be appeased, restitutions made, and usurpations redeemed. Such matters could not be arranged without long, and often harassing discussions. In the end, however, conciliation and impartial justice gained the day; and a reform, which in many cases ran counter to the interests and prejudices of the most powerful and refractory section of the community, was carried through without a shot being

[1] Ganesh is the first of the Hindu deities to be invoked and propitiated on every undertaking. The warrior implores his counsel; the banker indites his name at the commencement of his letters; the architect places his image in the foundation of every edifice; and the figure of Ganesh is either sculptured or painted at the door of every house as a protection against evil. He is four-armed, and holds the disc (chakra), the war-shell, the club, and the lotus. Nearly every Hindu city has a gate named after him, and his shrine will be found on the summit of every sacred hill. He is represented with an elephant's head and accompanied by a rat.

fired, or the exhibition of a single British soldier in the country.

The internal security which followed these reforms may be gaged from the fact that the rate of insurance on the transit of merchandise, which before the treaty had been eight per cent. for 25 miles, became almost nominal, or one-fourth of a rupee from one frontier to the other. As a specimen of the general progress, we may take the case of a single district, that of Shahára. Of its 27 villages, 6 were inhabited in 1818, the number of families being 369. In 1821, 926 families were reported, and every village of the 27 was occupied, so that population was almost trebled. The number of ploughs was more than trebled, and cultivation was quadrupled. The same ratio of prosperity applied to the entire crown demesne of Mewár.

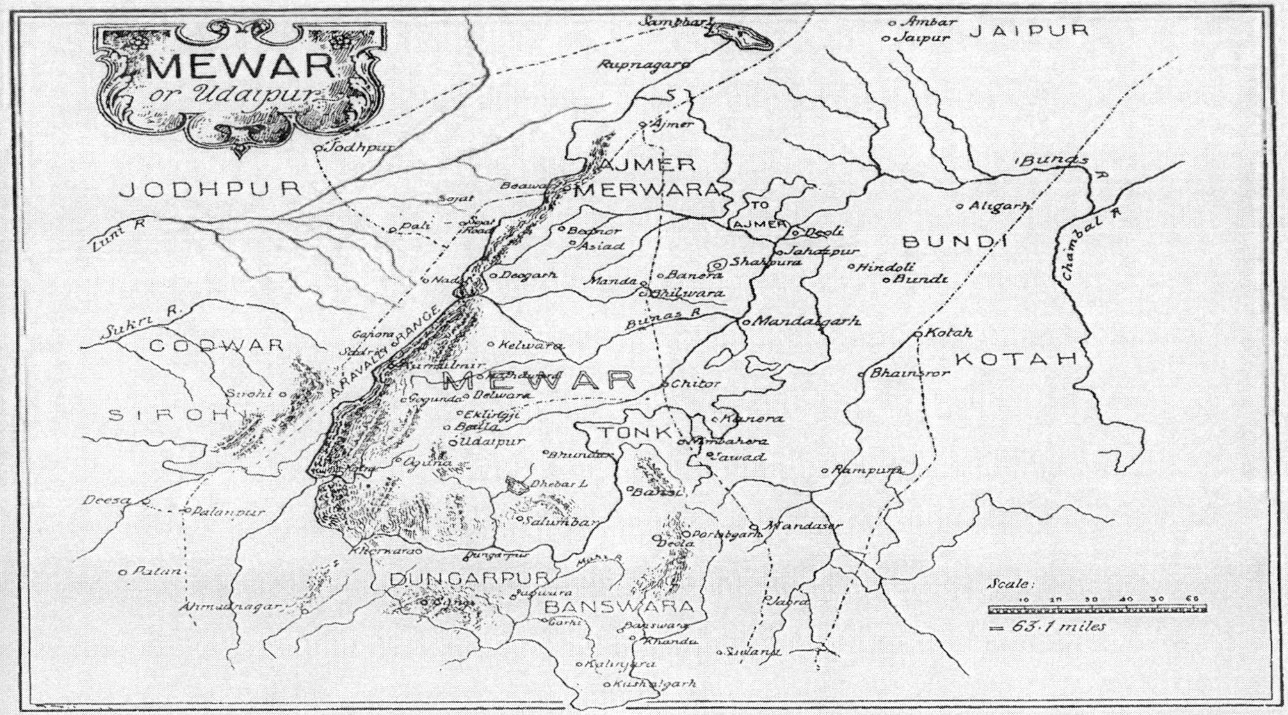
MEWAR
or Udaipur
JODHPUR
Jodhpur
JAIPUR
Ambar
Jaipur
Sambhar
Rupnagarh
Ajmer
AJMER
MERWARA
TO
AJMER
Deoli
Jahazpur
BUNDI
Aligarh
Bunas
Chambal R
Hindoli
Bundi
Kotah
KOTAH
Bhainsror
Rampura
Luni R
Pali
Sojat
Beawar
Badnor
Asind
Deogarh
Nadol
Banera
Manda
Bhilwara
Shahpura
Mandalgarh
Banas R
Sukri R
GODWAR
Ganora
Sadri
ARAVALLI RANGE
Kumbhalmir
Kelwara
MEWAR
Chitor
Sirohi
SIROHI
Gogunda
Delwara
Eklingji
Badla
Udaipur
TONK
Kanera
Nimbahera
Jawad
Bhindar
Dhebar L
Salumbar
Deesa
Palanpur
Patan
Kherwara
Dungarpur
DUNGARPUR
Mandasor
Partabgarh
Deola
Mahi R
BANSWARA
Sagwara
Garhi
Banswara
Khandu
Kushalgarh
Jaora
Sailana
Ahmednagar
Scale:
10 20 30 40 50 60
= 63.1 miles

Index